From Surviving
to Thriving

A Guide for Beginning Teachers

MARCIA BROMFIELD
LESLEY UNIVERSITY

HARRIET DEANE
LESLEY UNIVERSITY

ELLA BURNETT
CALIFORNIA STATE UNIVERSITY

Brookline Books
Brookline, Massachusetts 02445

This book is dedicated to all of the teachers who returned after their first year, in spite of the challenges, and who became the seasoned educators we know and respect. They are our inspiration.

To my husband Bruce Bordett, my daughter Sasha, and to my parents, Zangwill and the late Ruth Bromfield, with love and gratitude for all they have taught me and for their support and belief in what I could do. — *M.B.*

To my husband Ron, my daughter Laura, and to my parents, Lillian and Louis Deane, with love.   — *H.D.*

I owe my son Allen and my daughter Ashley and other family members for the many hours I spent focusing on my writing. I appreciate their encouragement and love throughout this project.   — *E.G B.*

ISBN 1-57129-092-3

Library of Congress Cataloging-In-Publication Data
Bromfield, Marcia.
  From surviving to thriving: a guide for beginning teachers / Marcia Bromfield, Harriet Deane, Ella Burnett.
  p. cm.
  ISBN 1-57129-092-3
  1. First year teachers--In-service training. 2. First year teachers--Professional relationships.
  I. Burnett, Ella. II. Deane, Harriet. III. Title.
  LB2844.1.N4B77 2003
  378.1'61'0973--dc21
                                 2003051865

Cover and interior design by Fish Tank Media

Printed in USA by P.A. Hutchison
10 9 8 7 6 5 4 3 2 1

Published by
BROOKLINE BOOKS
P.O. Box 97
Newton, MA 02464
Order toll-free: 1-800-666-BOOK

ACKNOWLEDGEMENTS

We have had the pleasure of working with thousands of aspiring and beginning teachers, veteran teachers and administrators, and teacher educators during our careers in education. They are excited about their chosen profession and eager to grow in their careers. We want to thank all of those who have talked to us and shared their questions and thoughts; our writing and our thinking have been informed by all of these conversations. We are grateful to have known so many caring, open, and professional individuals. Among those people, there are several who have given us specific support and input around the writing of this book, and we would like to acknowledge them here.

Some of the teachers who through conversations in groups, individually, or through written work have shared stories that we've used in various ways, are Abraham Abadi, Jennifer Arenson, Joanne Berger, Peter Bloom, Marie Lynch, and Roe Vickery. We also want to thank all of the teachers who have been participants in the beginning teacher groups which we've facilitated over the years, as well as those beginning and veteran teachers who generously allowed us to interview them and who spent time filling out our questionnaires.

Many of our insightful and dedicated practicum supervisors field-tested and commented on parts of the book. We are grateful to all of them, and want to give special thanks to Helen Budd, Ellie Gowen, Helen Novack, Debbie Perry, and Arlyn Roffman. Several other people generously spent time reading parts or all of the manuscript and giving us feedback at various stages. Their comments were invaluable in helping to refine and edit the book. Thank you to Emily Cross, Susan Daley, Jean Gumpert, Ron Koehler, Mary McMackin, Kim Rivers, and Annette Stavros.

During the preparation of this book, we worked with several graduate and research assistants who helped us in a variety of ways, such as collecting data through surveys and interviews, arranging and documenting beginning teacher support groups, and assisting with research and references. Without the many hours spent by Marcia Appell, Sandras Barnes, Peggy Burke, Emily Cross, and Susannah Horwitz, we would never have completed the book.

We received administrative and moral support from the administrative assistants in our office and want Joanne Bialoboki, Frances Danilkin, Jeannette Hyatt, and Emily Minty to know that we appreciate them.

We are also grateful for the support we received from the Faculty Development Grant Program and the Russell Fellowship Program at Lesley University, which provided resources to help us facilitate the beginning teacher groups and to do our research. Writing retreats, sponsored by Lesley University and facilitated by Winnie Skolnikoff, Donna Cole, and Solange Lira, provided us with time to think, encouragement, and helpful feedback.

Bruce Bordett and Ron Koehler gave us technical assistance, moral support, and gentle nudging, and for this and more, we thank them.

We are very grateful to Margery Miller, our friend and colleague, who as acting dean when we began this book, encouraged us to begin, and to Bill Dandridge, our current dean, who always supported us and encouraged us to finish.

Our publisher and editor, Milt Budoff, spent countless hours discussing ideas and concepts, gave us feedback on many drafts, and painstakingly went over every word with us. We truly appreciate his patience, persistence, and wise counsel.

We want to thank all of our colleagues, friends, and families for listening to us talk about this book for many years, for giving us ideas, and for believing that we could actually complete it. Without our networks of wonderful people, we would never have written this book!

TABLE OF CONTENTS

PREFACE

Today the profession of education is in constant change, and nothing has changed so dramatically as the role of the teacher. It is much less common for a teacher to close her door and be the only adult in the classroom all day. Teachers need to know how to collaborate and coordinate with aides, specialists, special educators, administrators and other school staff, and to understand the school as an organization with a distinct culture. Of course it is also essential that collaborative relationships extend to students, parents, and the community as well. In an increasingly diverse society, it is more important than ever for teachers to be able to communicate with students and families who come from a variety of cultures with differing understandings and expectations. Finally, the constant change in education and society at large requires that teachers themselves are continuous learners and that they take charge of their own professional development. The world of teaching is becoming a much different place than it has traditionally been.

This change has revolutionary opportunities and implications for teachers, parents, and their students. This book, which primarily seeks to provide support to new teachers and help student teachers understand these changes in classrooms, provides valuable guidance in areas not usually addressed in teacher training programs, though the academic and practice literature is very concerned about them.

A major goal for all teacher education programs is to prepare their graduates for "good beginnings with children, colleagues, administration, and community." The authors note, that in our focus on ensuring our graduates, readiness to work with children, too little attention is paid to their understanding of the complex organizational structure in which they work and the social relationships that exist among the adult members of the school community: the challenge described by Roland Barth that "much that is important is unwritten."

From Surviving to Thriving offers important insights into the social, political, and power relationships within schools. The authors provide critical observations and case examples based on their more than ninety years of experience to help the beginning teacher identify and to make explicit these important factors that are not written or shared in public. They acknowledge the challenges when entering a close-knit community where there are unspoken understandings about decision-making, norms, values, and relationships. A major emphasis is "colleagues matter" for support, as collaborators in teaching and planning curricula, and to sharpen one's teaching. The text is full of thoughtful suggestions to help the new teacher to observe, analyze, and understand the events around him in the school. There are exercises that offer the new teacher-reader opportunities to increase their awareness and understanding of their new school community. These skills are useful in many different situations and settings.

The authors focus on four major themes that they believe are essential in moving from surviving to thriving. The reader is encouraged to pay attention to culture, community, collaboration, and professional growth and development.

The ultimate goal of the book is to support and enrich the life of the new teacher so she stays as a teacher beyond the initial three years. The book is designed and intended to serve as a career long reference, a guide to assist in meeting new challenges and, most important, to be a supportive companion that should be consulted frequently.

William Dandridge, Dean of Education
LESLEY UNIVERSITY

CHAPTER ONE

INTRODUCTION

My experience suggests that the professional growth of teachers is closely related to relationships within schools, between teacher and principal, and between teacher and teacher. (Barth, 1990, p.50)

As we move into the twenty-first century, schools are changing dramatically, and the roles of teachers are changing as well. As a new teacher, you cannot expect to come into your classroom and close the door. You need to not only know how to teach children; you must be able to interact with, learn from, and mentor other adults as well. Of course, we know that a teacher must feel comfortable with her knowledge of content and pedagogy. She must have a command of the subject matter as well as teaching strategies, curriculum and assessment, behavior and classroom management. Without a firm grounding in all of these areas, you can't even step into a classroom. However, since these issues are discussed in preservice education programs and in many other books for new teachers, we've chosen not to address them in this book. Even if one has mastered the basics of successful teaching, lack of attention to the norms and practices of the larger school community can lead to isolation and defeat.

Schools now are very complicated places. Contrary to what has been true in the past, few teachers today are alone in their classrooms. Often several adults go in and out of a classroom every day. You may be a special education teacher or other specialist who does this yourself. In order to meet the complex needs of children and the call for public accountability, you must interact effectively with many other adults — parents, teachers, specialists, administrators, and other staff. Also, the information age has brought communication to a new level. Instant access is expected, and many opportunities for global and local sharing of information and ideas are available. We wish to help teachers to understand these forces beyond the classroom and to reflect on ways to turn them into assets, using a proactive, rather than a reactive approach. We want to help teachers learn how to work with other adults to better serve their own needs, the needs of their students, and the larger school.

To implement new ideas and to enhance teaching practices, professional development is critical, especially for beginning teachers. As we have learned more about professional development, we know that what is most effective are not the formal workshops given by school systems, not the presentations by experts, but ongoing, practice-based support. This kind of support can often be found within your school or district. Your colleagues who know the children, the community, the curriculum, and the culture may be your best source of professional development. Colleagues in other systems can also share knowledge and ideas which are invaluable. It's up to you to seek them out and create your own personal plan for learning. By giving you ideas to help you learn about the culture of your school and how to work with other adults, we hope to help you to seek the support you'll need to develop and promote your own plan for professional development.

Beginning teaching is often marked by feelings of personal and professional isolation, which can contribute significantly to the stresses and challenges. Too often this isolation leads to leaving the profession. Figuring out how best to work with others will help combat these feelings. For many reasons then, it's becoming increasingly clear that in order to become a successful professional teacher, you need to understand that your colleagues matter in your practice.

Our combined experience of over 90 years as classroom teachers, teacher educators, supervisors of student teachers, and a field placement director has enabled us to see first hand the content and strengths, as well as the gaps, in teacher preparation programs. We have talked to and taught thousands of preservice and beginning teachers, working primarily in elementary and middle schools, in general education and special education. In addition, in preparation for this book, we have facilitated support groups, distributed and analyzed surveys, and interviewed beginning teachers. In our experience and the opinions of those with whom we've talked, the topics included in this book, which are directly related to issues of culture, community, collaboration, and professional growth and development tend to be neglected in teacher preparation programs. Even if they are discussed in a course or seminar, these topics tend to be ignored or seen as unimportant, compared to the day to day realities of managing one's own classroom. New teachers need to understand that much that is important in schools is unwritten. We want to help you to decipher those aspects of the setting which might not be obvious.

We chose these topics in order to help beginning teachers and student teachers, particularly in elementary and middle schools, usefully understand the work settings of their schools and classrooms and their relationships with colleagues. Our goals for this book are:

1. To enable beginning teachers to survive their first years of teaching and student teachers to be better prepared for this year, and

2. To help these initiates build the base on which they can grow personally and professionally, as they embrace their new profession.

WHAT IS A PROFESSIONAL TEACHER?

You must come to view yourself and act as a professional. Much has been written about the profession of teaching over the past fifteen years, and there have been several major reports calling for "professionalizing" teaching. What does it mean to be a professional teacher? What are the standards of the profession and the complex roles that professional teachers assume?

1. Your college education, your liberal arts studies and professional education in content areas and pedagogy, your field experiences, internships, involvement in community work, and your beginning years of teaching experience are the foundation for becoming a professional. A professional teacher is well-grounded in the content knowledge and ways of thinking of the disciplines she is teaching. A professional is always striving to live up to a high standard, has a commitment to lifelong learning, and possesses the desire to continue growing and evolving in her chosen field. A professional teacher develops a knowledge and experience base, as well as professional judgment with which to evaluate and weigh new information and teaching strategies for each student in her class.

2. A professional teacher advocates for his students. To be an effective advocate, a professional teacher needs to know how to communicate effectively with children and adults in the classroom, school, district, and community and knows how to access resources and support services from other professionals and staff members within the school and

the wider community. As a teacher you learn the boundaries and limits of your role, and know when to refer students and families to other professionals. You have to accept that you may have to work with situations that are less than ideal. You will need to remain proactive and advocate in as positive a way as possible. You will develop your skills as a creative problem solver.

3. A professional teacher maintains high ethical standards. Several of the major professional teaching organizations have developed ethical standards for the profession. For example, the National Association for the Education of Young Children (NAEYC) has developed its Code of Ethical Conduct and Statement of Commitment. NAEYC encourages early childhood educators to strive to uphold these standards and engage in discussions of the moral dilemmas that can occur in their work with children and families. The Council for Exceptional Children (CEC) has also developed a code of ethics, which should be upheld by special education professionals. The NAEYC Journal often includes a section that discusses some of the ethical dilemmas that occur in practice and gives examples of how teachers can use the ethical standards as guidelines to develop responses to complex issues. Many professional organizations also publish standards of practice and position statements on controversial issues. For example, NAEYC has published position papers on issues such as child abuse and early literacy development, and CEC has developed standards of practice in areas such as advocacy and behavior management. These professional position statements and standards can support you in your daily work.

Some ethical issues, such as confidentiality, are generic to many professions. As a teacher, you will be privy to highly confidential information regarding children and families. You need to know under what circumstances this information can be shared and need to be cognizant of protecting private information. As a professional teacher, you will continuously strive to demonstrate good judgment in difficult situations. You will want to avoid contributing to rumors and conversations that show disrespect for other teachers, children, or families in the community. As tempting as it is to vent and blow off steam when you work in a highly interactive profession, you will monitor your responses and conversation when they involve confidential information.

4. As you evolve as a professional, you will learn to confront your own biases and prejudices. Your goals will include eliminating behaviors

that imply attitudes of racism, sexism, handicapism, classism or homophobia. As you work with a diverse group of colleagues, students, and families, you will make mistakes and may occasionally cause hurt feelings because of your lack of knowledge. A respect for others and an honest apology and effort to learn about other perspectives goes a long way. You will continuously strive to expand your knowledge and understanding of the diversity in our society in terms of race, class, gender, and language differences. As a professional, it is critical to develop an understanding of your own cultural background and the perspectives that you bring to your work. As you grow in your understanding of diversity, of specific knowledge of different cultures, and of the history of different cultural groups in this country, you will be able to look at a situation from different perspectives and will be more effective in understanding points of view that differ from your own.

SUGGESTIONS FOR USING THIS GUIDE

Throughout this book, we provide suggested exercises, vignettes, forms for reflection and other types of guides to assist you in structuring and recording your experience in the schools. The issues we've selected have emerged from concerns and stories of the student teachers and beginning teachers with whom we've worked. We explore strategies for understanding school cultures, gaining support, and working with various constituencies in the larger school community. We present exercises, based on authentic stories from teachers, to help you think about teaching.

Develop a Journal for Each Year's Teaching

To maximize the usefulness of this guide, you should keep a journal, where you can jot down ideas and thoughts, record your responses to the exercises, and look at your development over time. The exercises and vignettes in the book will be most useful to you if you write your responses. Reading the questions and answering them yourself without this writing process will not be as helpful later. If you write them down, you can see what you were thinking and remind yourself of what happened during the earlier days of the year. You will want to select those exercises and answer those questions that are relevant to you and/or are assigned by your supervisor if you are a student teacher.

Although we are aware that you may be overwhelmed by all of the demands you are now facing, we have learned from experience that writing down your thoughts will be well worth the effort. For example, your early impressions of your school can tell you a lot about how it feels to others who enter the building. This feeling may impact the way children and families view coming to the school. Only by writing will you remember your impressions and thoughts of the first couple of weeks. You don't need to write every night, but a couple of times a week will be very helpful.

As a possible format for your general writing, one approach might be to set up each entry in your journal as high points, low points, insights, reflections, and questions. Long, involved descriptions of your day might be too tedious, time-consuming, and repetitious. In later reviews of your journal, you can see how and whether your views have changed. Keeping your journal where you can jot down your ideas and thoughts maximizes the utility of this guide. But we don't want your journal writing to be burdensome. You want it to give you the opportunity for thoughtful reflection on your experience over time.

We have written this book with two major audiences in mind — pre-service candidates currently in practicum placements and beginning teachers. Since the demands on these two groups differ, we expect that each group might use this book differently.

For The Beginning Teacher:

Although we believe that it is valuable for all educators to keep a journal, we understand that when you are coping with the many demands of beginning teaching, you may not find the time to do all of the exercises. We certainly don't want to add to your stress level! We suggest that you pick and choose; try to decide which areas of the book will be most helpful to you at any particular time and choose to do those exercises that will help you in dealing with issues that you are facing.

If you're not sure where to begin, we suggest that you start with Chapter Two, so that you can systematically orient yourself to your new school. You might want to also read Chapter Three before school starts, since it will give you ideas about how to begin to get to know your students, even before the first day. Chapter Four should be read early, because it provides suggestions about ways of working with families and approaching your first Open School Night, all of which will be important from the start of the year. You might want to read Chapters Eight and Six next. Chapter Eight on avoiding burnout will, hopefully, help you to handle some of the inevitable stresses of the first year. Chapter Six will assist you in understanding and developing collegial relationships, which will be critical to your success, and will also reduce stress, especially in the early years. The remaining chapters can be read as you have the time and energy.

For the Student Teacher:

We expect that you may do more of these exercises. Many student teaching experiences are accompanied by a seminar, which serves as an opportunity to collectively reflect on day-to-day experiences in classrooms and schools. These experiential discussions are essential to helping students sort out and make sense of the many things they are learning. The themes addressed in the book can be incorporated into a weekly seminar to lend a structure to experiential discussions and to provide tools for reflection. We also hope to be able to assist student teachers in reconciling the realities of the classroom with the theories and ideas learned in preservice courses. The exercises can help focus your reflections and guide your discussions. Most likely, the instructor of your seminar will assign chapters and exercises as appropriate.

OVERVIEW OF CHAPTERS

The key concepts we believe are most important for beginning teaching are interwoven throughout this book. These concepts, listed below, are often overlooked by beginning teachers but are crucial to successfully learning how to teach:

- ❏ understanding your school culture can be critical to your professional development and takes time and effort;
- ❏ to truly know and understand your students, you must learn about their lives outside as well as inside the classroom and the school;
- ❏ building collegial connections with other adults within and outside the school is important to your success;
- ❏ including your personal as well as professional self in your priorities will enhance your success.

Using these key concepts, we will guide you toward developing personal and professional goals that will increase your chances of successfully navigating the first few years of teaching.

Chapter Two, which deals with observing and understanding the culture of the school, provides you with guidelines for understanding the norms and expectations in the setting and observing the formal and informal ways in which teachers, administrators, and staff function and interact. Using exercises for your journal will help you learn about these issues and develop effective strategies for understanding and functioning within your school's culture.

Chapter Three focuses on the learners in your classroom. Interest in students is the reason most elementary and middle school teachers enter the profession. The learners in your room spend as many waking hours outside of school as they do inside. To successfully teach each child, you will want to get to know each child as a whole person. We suggest ways that you can find out what is important to the child and who the significant adults are who influence her. We'll help you think about how you can get to know the temperament and personality of each individual. "Getting to know your students" provides you with suggestions for gauging each child's learning and learning-related behaviors, which help you develop better ways of relating to the children and meeting their academic and emotional needs. One of your biggest challenges will be to integrate the information you gather about individual children so that you can nurture a classroom climate that supports diversity.

Chapters Four and Five, on your students' families and the community surrounding the school respectively enable you to explore the contexts of your students' lives outside the school. Building relationships and communicating with families and others in the community will enhance success in the classroom. In these two chapters, we discuss ways of fostering and encouraging family participation in the learning process, and multiple ways of developing home/school/community connections. Awareness of the changing demographics of family life and the range of family structures in the United States in the twenty-first century will assist you in developing strong and meaningful partnerships with the families of your students, a major goal today. As you begin to define what constitutes your own particular school community, you should explore a wide range of community resources, develop linkages to community agencies, discover existing school/college/business partnerships and develop opportunities for involvement in learning activities within the community.

Chapter Six focuses on working with colleagues and gives suggestions for ways to connect with other professionals. Besides developing relationships with students, relationships with other adults are essential to the success of beginning teachers. We address mentoring and explore ways in which both formal and informal mentors can be helpful to you during your beginning years of teaching. We outline strategies for building relationships with other classroom teachers and specialists to enhance the learning of the children in your room. We discuss some of the collegial models you may experience in your school setting, such as co-teaching, peer coaching, and teaming. We also address some of the issues that may occur when you are working with other adults, such as aides or assistants, in your own classroom. Finally, we talk about potential conflicts that might arise when working with the other adults in your settings and suggest some ways of addressing these conflicts.

Chapter Seven focuses on guiding you through a process of reflection and self-evaluation, which will lead you towards professional growth and self-renewal. We will introduce you to various tools which will help you reflect on your practice and support your lifelong learning. Although much of your reflection may occur informally, such structured techniques as journals, portfolios, classroom inquiry/action research, and soliciting feedback from others can help you to more systematically look at your teaching. These varied avenues to reflection can be used at different points in your career, depending on your time and inclination. Journals and portfolios are often required in teacher preparation programs, and you may be comfortable beginning with these as tools for reflection. Conducting action research in your classroom can help you gain insights about the curriculum and your teaching. Getting feedback from others to aid in your reflections can be very helpful and rewarding too. The different perspectives of supervisors, peers, or students can give you much needed insight into your successes and challenges. Successful teachers begin the process of reflection in various ways when they begin teaching and continue to develop this skill throughout the rest of their careers.

In Chapter Eight, we remind you that you have to take care of yourself. Although this concept is at the end of the list, sometimes you will have to put yourself first. Chapter Eight discusses avoiding burnout. It will help you become more sensitive to your expectations and those of others and sustain your professional growth. We encourage you to accept the fact that you cannot do everything you want to the first year. Expect to experience disappointment and frustration, even after your best efforts. You will then be more likely to succeed in dealing with stress and avoid burnout.

This chapter stresses the importance of staying mentally and physically fit in order to keep up with the rigor of teaching. We encourage you to focus on yourself and your own needs: to get sufficient rest, eat right, and carve out some leisure time. We suggest that even if you have family members who count on you, they will benefit in the long run if you take good care of yourself. In this chapter, we advise that, in spite of the many demands on you in your first years of teaching, you need to work for balance in life. We'll help you think about what you need to do to take care of yourself personally and to find satisfaction professionally.

In the last chapter, we explore the variety of professional communities that provide support and professional development to new and veteran teachers. You will be reminded that you most likely have many choices for your formal professional development. Your school and district will provide some sort of orientation and periodic workshops and training sessions. You can also attend conferences of professional organizations, take courses at a college or university, and study on your own. You are the best individual to be in charge of your development professionally. It's important that you assess and consciously develop your own teaching skills throughout your teaching career. Many of the ideas discussed in this book, such as creating and maintaining a portfolio, taking advantage of peer coaching, networking with others, or reading education journals, will help you to monitor your growth and development as a professional.

As you read through the rest of this book, we hope that you'll find ideas that will encourage you to think about your experience in new ways. We hope that our suggestions will help you to understand your school, to learn to work with your colleagues in productive and enjoyable ways, and to gain the confidence you need to continue to grow as a teacher.

We hope that you will see this as a useful guidebook that you'll want to pick up and read in sections when you have a specific question or concern. Keep it by your bedside, carry it in your briefcase, put it in your desk. However you use it, we hope that it will help you to think about and come up with solutions to some of those unanswered questions, those sticky issues, those mysteries of the teaching profession, that you just hadn't considered before. We hope that this book will help ease your way as you begin this most important, most challenging, most satisfying career. We wish you many years of successful teaching!

Suggested Resources

Ayers, W. (1993). *To teach: The journey of a teacher.* New York: Teachers College Press.

Ayers, W. (Ed.), (1995). *To become a teacher: Making a difference in children's lives.* New York: Teacher's College Press.

Fried, R.L. (1995). *The passionate teacher.* Boston: Beacon Press.

Sarason, S. (1993). *You are thinking of teaching? Opportunities, problems, realities.* John Wiley& Sons.

CHAPTER TWO

LEARNING ABOUT YOUR SCHOOL

It comes as no surprise to learn that teachers are happier working in some schools and districts than in others. Pleasant surroundings, cooperative relationships, manageable workloads, and ample resources promote greater satisfaction than do dreary buildings, hostile social climates, excessive demands and inadequate resources. But what is often overlooked or discounted by those who want good schools is that the character of the school as a workplace affects not only the satisfaction of faculty, but the work that even the most talented, highly motivated, well-intentioned teachers can do. (Johnson, 1990, p.10)

Even though your first priority as a new teacher is to teach the children in your class, to really be successful you need to do more than go into your classroom and close the door. Every school, like every other organization, has its own culture. As a new teacher, it is critical to understand the norms, expectations, values, and interpersonal dynamics of the school where you are teaching. It won't be easy to figure all of this out. No one will hand you a manual or a rulebook that tells you exactly how this particular school works, how things really get done, and to whom you can safely go for help and support. As one veteran teacher, recently beginning a job in a new school said, "My greatest problem is the "secrets" in the school. The principal and most of the faculty have been here many years. Many of the traditions and ways of doing things were never explained to me" (Brock & Grady, 1997, P. 24). You may identify with this statement. Every school has its secrets, and in this chapter, we will try to help you figure out how to learn the "secrets" in your school.

Most people entering teaching seem to fall back on their own experiences as students. As a new teacher, you need to have a more complete sense of how a school operates than your own early experiences would give you. This chapter seeks to broaden that perspective by giving you ideas and tools to help you look at different aspects of your school and understand how it functions. Even if you're an experienced teacher, if you are beginning in a new school, you won't know how things work. Although there are similarities among schools, there are also many differences. The culture of a particular school is defined by the leadership of the school, the interpersonal relationships and interactions among the people in the school, the personalities of those people, the academic orientation, the influences and interests of peer groups, the total context of the school (Lieberman & Miller, 1992). Most likely no one will sit you down and explain these things to you. You'll need to figure them out for yourself — and the sooner the better! The more intentionally you watch and listen to the life of the school, the more successful will be your adjustment to your first year and the better off you'll be.

So why would you want to learn about your school? You may be asking, "What do you mean by culture, and how will understanding the school culture help me to be a better teacher?" Let's think about this for a minute.

> We use the concept "culture" to refer to the guiding beliefs and expectations evident in the way a school operates, particularly in reference to how people relate (or fail to relate) to each other. In simple terms, culture is "the way we do things and relate to each other around here." (Fullan & Hargreaves, 1996, p.37)

Your life will be easier if you learn about general procedures as well as where you need to go to get things done. Also, even if you have graduated from an excellent teacher preparation program, you won't know everything about teaching. It is helpful to know whom you can safely approach for advice, support, or ideas. Another important reason is that knowing about your school will help you to clarify your own values and determine your own goals as a professional teacher. Observing what is going on in your school will help you to tell whether your professional goals, motivation, and style are compatible with those of your colleagues and will help you to develop your own style and teaching practices. You'll need to think about how to enter this new environment in a way that allows you to keep your ideas and still work within the culture that exists. Do your own personal and professional values blend with what you see in your school? How do you think you'll be able to operate within this particular culture?

You won't be able to understand your school in a day or two. We are advocating a long, careful study. You don't want to misread a situation and do something you'll regret later. If you look and listen carefully, in a month or two you'll have a better idea of who the players are, what are some of the unwritten rules, and how people interact. It will probably take at least three to six months to really begin to understand the dynamics of this unique environment that is your school.

There are several key aspects of a school that you should try to learn about in order to help you understand the culture. The culture of a school is a complex combination of several features, such as:

- ❏ the physical building and facilities;
- ❏ the systems of leadership and decision-making;
- ❏ the demographics of staff, students,and community;
- ❏ the collegiality and interactions among teachers, administrators, students, and others;
- ❏ family issues and interactions between families and staff;
- ❏ shared traditions and purposes;
- ❏ core values;
- ❏ professional development opportunities;
- ❏ external partnerships and the relationship of the school to the community.

In this chapter, we'll discuss these features and suggest some exercises for your journal which will help you structure a picture of your school.

As you write in your journal, we recommend that you do the exercises and answer those questions that you are able to answer and that seem most relevant to you. As you go through the year, you may want to go back to these exercises, read and reflect on what you wrote initially, and perhaps respond to those most relevant to you again. Hence, you may want to do some of the exercises first at the beginning of the year, again around mid-year, and, if you have time, again in May or during the summer to see the fuller picture over time. Responding to the questions will help you to frame your thinking about what you are seeing and experiencing in your school.

You may get your answers in many ways. Observe carefully in all situations. Watch for seating patterns and speaking patterns in classrooms and meeting rooms, topics of conversation, signs, posters, decorations, room setup and location. Keep your eyes and ears open, and you will learn what really makes your school the unique place it is!

You might think about getting to know your school in two stages. Your first impressions of the school will be based on the physical environment. What does the school look like when you first see it? When you drive or walk up to the building, what are the first thoughts that cross your mind? Does the building give you a sense of a place that is cared for and attractive, or does it feel like a place that nobody cares about and where nothing has been done for years? Is it clean and landscaped, or are there broken windows and trash littering the area? The appearance of the building does give a message about what the school might be like as an environment for work and learning. Think about how you will feel going into the building every day. The first part of this chapter addresses these issues of the physical setting and helps you to think about what it might mean for your teaching.

The second stage of understanding your school involves aspects of the environment which are more related to the people inside, such as getting to know who they are and how they relate to each other. Some of these aspects of the school include the norms of the school, relationships that exist and are expected among colleagues and with families, and expectations of the leadership. You can't learn about these issues until you are working there, observing and listening to what is going on. As you become part of the staff, you should think about how the school feels, both as a learning environment and a workplace.

ENTERING THE CULTURE

> *A school's culture is not something that the school possesses. Instead the culture is its very essence, a tapestry of meanings developed throughout the years of the school's existence.* (Brock & Grady, p. 52)

As you enter your new school, with all the exciting ideas you have learned in your teacher preparation program, it will be easy to see what is right and wrong with the school. Be careful to suspend judgment. Take the time to observe, to learn the history behind specific practices. Try not to alienate your colleagues by being too quick to offer simple solutions to ongoing problems. The issues may be much more complicated than you think. If you act like a know-it-all, you will most likely turn people off. If you suggest ideas that seem obvious, you can easily give the impression that you think your colleagues lack insight. As a new person in the school, you need to respect the knowledge of those who are already there. Remember that no situation is perfect, and no one lives in the best of all possible worlds. You need to be able to adjust to different types of situations and learn to see the positive aspects of your colleagues and their teaching. Especially as a new teacher, you have something to learn from each of them. Try to get to know them and to make a sincere effort to find out their strengths and their areas of expertise. You will probably find that you can benefit greatly from the knowledge that they are willing to share with you.

As a new teacher, you may not yet understand the perspectives of more experienced teachers. You may have come out of a supportive teacher preparation program where you had opportunities to discuss issues with faculty and fellow classmates. Some of your discussions may have even focused on what's wrong with the current educational system and ways in which you can be a change agent. You may see yourself as part of the educational reform movement. These are noble and important perspectives, and we aren't advocating that you become isolated or give up your ideals. Since they may not be shared by your teacher colleagues and administrators, we are merely advising you to proceed with caution.

You are more likely to receive support for your ideas if you first become accepted by your colleagues than if you are perceived as an idealistic outsider. Teachers often feel that they aren't consulted about educational change and that change is often forced on them. At various times in our society, they are the victims of teacher-bashing. You don't want to feed into those feelings among experienced teachers in your school. If your ideas differ significantly from the norms in the rest of the school, even if you do not want to change others, but only want to practice your own ways of teaching, you'll want to gain support from your peers. The purpose of this chapter is not to give you the ammunition and a license to criticize, but to help you determine how to gain the information and support that will help you to survive and thrive during that crucial first year.

PHYSICAL ENVIRONMENT

The physical features of schools affect both the circumstances and the substance of schooling — what it is like to teach and learn as well as what can be taught and learned. (Johnson, 1990, p.58)

What was your reaction when you entered your school for the first time? Did it feel welcoming or was it cold and unfriendly? The physical environment of a school clearly affects the feelings and behaviors of everyone who spends time in the building—teachers and other staff, parents, and children. People can be made to feel valued or devalued by the condition of their environment. We don't always realize the impact of the physical setting on the way we feel about and do our jobs. Although these effects may be subtle, they are very real. Some of the important aspects of the physical environment are:

- ❑ the architecture of the building itself;
- ❑ the condition and maintenance of the physical plant;
- ❑ attention to safety and security;
- ❑ availability of teaching supplies; and
- ❑ the ways in which people have affected the environment by decorating and furnishing their rooms, the halls, and other areas.

We suggest that you observe the physical setting of the building itself. Look at maintenance and cleanliness, as well as aesthetics. Think about whether it's an attractive, welcoming place. Look at the way space inside the school is being and might be used. Try to see what kinds of materials and equipment are available to students and teachers. Think about what the physical setting says about respect for the people inside, their values, and the community.

You will want to look at the kinds of spaces there are in the school. Space can impose limits or facilitate flexibility. Limitations of space may be most troubling to the most creative teachers. Movement, grouping, and diverse methodologies require a physical environment which is conducive to such activities. Try not to get discouraged though, if you are faced with a less than ideal physical setting. Don't forget that there might be ways to deal with these issues. Furniture can usually be rearranged; spend some time thinking about how you want it to be in order to facilitate the activities you want to do, and consult with more experienced colleagues.

The architecture of a building can encourage collegiality and collaboration or isolation. For example, we know of one brand new school that is strikingly beautiful, with bright colors, lovely design features, ample-sized classrooms, but where the layout of the halls makes it difficult for teachers to see each other, unless they go out of their way to do so. Teachers have said that they feel more isolated than they did in their shabby old building. Look at what kinds of non-classroom space there are in your school. If there are no meeting rooms and few common areas, collaboration is discouraged. However, there may be ways to motivate people to go out of their way to meet. Even as a new teacher, you might be able to help this happen. Bringing food and inviting people to come to your room or another room after school might encourage informal conversation, for example.

So what do you do if the physical environment is less than ideal? You may need to think creatively about how to design a positive, welcoming environment in your own classroom and even elsewhere in the school. Perhaps you can find colleagues, parents, or other community volunteers who would like to work with you to make your surroundings more pleasant. It's important to consider the attitudes of others towards your efforts. You can make improvements in ways that alienate others or in ways that improve the morale of those around you and are appreciated. Learn to be creative and to brainstorm with like-minded colleagues about possible ways around the physical limitations of your school. These brainstorming discussions can be yet another chance to talk about teaching and build collegial relationships. Think about what you have learned from your analysis of the culture, about how the school and how the faculty will regard these efforts before you forge ahead.

2.1 Exercise for Your Journal:
Looking at Space in the School

Sketch the physical layout of your school. Look at different types of spaces, as well as where classroom and other spaces are located in relation to each other. Indicate the access from one space to another. Think about how the physical layout and space might affect teaching and working with others. Some specific questions to consider are:

- Are there large spaces where classes could combine for activities?
- Do teachers have easy access to each others' classrooms? Are classrooms connected in any way?
- Which classes are in proximity to each other? How might the location affect teaming and co-teaching?

- Are special education classes located near other classes of similar grade level?
- Where are specialists located?
- Are there meeting rooms of various sizes where teachers (or other community members) could meet and work together?
- Is there space for parents to congregate?

As you observe the physical environment of the school, think about how the availability of supplies and materials might affect your teaching. Teachers need adequate materials in order to implement exciting and innovative curriculum. Although creative teachers make some of their own materials, they need to have the supplies to use. They also can't spend inordinate amounts of time constructing materials. Some new teachers may find themselves spending so much time trying to make materials that they may have little energy left for working with children. The most creative teachers may need the greatest range of supplies. A teacher who teaches from texts only, or a teacher who teaches the same lessons year after year may make do with less. "Deficits in space and supplies are not only indignities and inconveniences; they compromise the efforts and efficacy of even, and perhaps, especially, the best teachers. . . . Good teachers thrive when they work in good spaces with sufficient supplies" (Johnson, p.59)

What if you are in a school that lacks supplies? You can learn to scrounge for materials; many factories and businesses may be willing to donate materials to schools. You might request donations yourself, get parents to ask, or, even better, turn the request into a lesson for your children, integrating it into language arts, math, or other areas of the curriculum. You might also write grants for materials. By working with colleagues, you can support each other in working on grants, while also creating opportunities for conversations about your teaching. If your school has a partnership with a college or business, look to them for possible resources.

"Materials and the procedures used to order them can influence teaching. Inadequate materials and ordering procedures discourage creativity. Encouraging teachers to purchase supplies together seems to promote collegial interaction" (Johnson, p.72). When teachers have conversations about supplies and materials, they will generally also discuss why they need particular materials; thus they will talk about their curriculum and what goes on in their classrooms. These discussions can lead to sharing and collaborative curriculum planning.

2.2 Exercise for Your Journal: How Do I Get Materials?

When you enter your new classroom for the first time, you may find that it seems almost empty. It will be very important for you to learn how you can access materials. During the first month of teaching, find out what materials are available and how materials are ordered. Speak to several teachers, as well as the secretary and administrators about this. Use the following questions as a guide and note the answers in your journal.

- Are there materials available and easily accessed? Where and how? What kind?
- Do teachers feel that they have adequate materials to do their jobs well?
- Do teachers influence the ordering of materials? Is ordering materials a difficult process? How is it done?
- Can necessary materials be ordered as needed, or must they be ordered well in advance?
- Do teachers spend their own money buying supplies? How do they feel about this?
- Does the PTA provide any funds for materials and supplies? How is this accessed and distributed?

LEADERSHIP AND DECISION-MAKING

What would happen if, in addition to becoming a community of learners, the new 'school' were to become a community of 'leaders?'. . . And how much richer the experience of all inhabitants of the learning community would be if each were expected to, allowed to, and helped to make decisions leading to the ongoing development of a community of learners and leaders. Leadership is making happen what you believe in. A school can accomplish no higher goal than to empower everyone— students, teachers, administrators, parents — with the confidence and ability to make happen what they believe in. (Barth, 1996, p.7)

Make sure that you pay attention to the ways that leadership functions in your building. You'll soon see that the atmosphere in a school is clearly influenced by the principal. She can set a tone that affects morale of teachers either positively or negatively.

> The principal has the power to make working in a school pleasant or unbearable; . . . A principal who makes teaching pleasant is one who trusts the staff to perform classroom duties with competence, and who deals with parents and the community in a way that supports teachers' decisions and safeguards against personal attacks. (Lieberman & Miller, 1992, P.12)

The principal can create an environment that is supportive or punitive. If the principal is perceived as critical, teachers will be less likely to want to try new approaches. When the principal is viewed as supportive, teachers will be more likely to take risks, to try new and creative approaches (Lieberman & Miller, 1992). You will probably feel more comfortable asking for resources and permission to do special activities if you see your principal as supportive.

As a new teacher, try to listen carefully to the ways in which teachers talk about the principal, and observe the behavior of the principal with other teachers, both in informal interactions and in meetings. Your ability to meet the expectations of the principal will clearly influence your success. Think carefully about how you'll approach both your colleagues and the principal with your ideas.

Decisions in schools are made in many different ways. In some schools the principal is the only one who makes decisions. In other schools, teachers and other staff take leadership roles and share in the responsibility for decision-making. If there's an assistant principal, what is her role? A principal who is comfortable with shared leadership can nurture the leadership growth of others. Of course, the nature of the decision will affect the way it is made. For example, core values, discussed later in this chapter, are expected to be modelled and instilled in the school community as a whole, both at home and at school. Thus you would expect that decisions about core values would generally be made through a broadly participatory process. The ways in which decisions are made will be closely linked to the nature of leadership in the school. If the principal is an authoritarian leader, for example, one would expect him to make decisions without consulting others. Think about how you define your role in such a school.

In some schools, there's a strong committee structure. Standing committees may deal with ongoing issues such as professional development or personnel; ad hoc committees may address specific, time-limited issues, such as implementation of a particular curriculum or planning of an event. Other committees may grapple with issues and then advise the leadership. Some decisions may be based in the school, and others may be more centralized in the district or even at the state level. Many states have legislated school councils, including school and community representatives, that advise the principal on critical issues.

**2.3 Exercise for Your Journal:
       Observations at Meetings**

One way to determine how decisions are made, how leadership functions, and who has influence in a school is to observe at various meetings. You won't be able to get a clear picture from one meeting, so try to observe carefully at a minimum of two or three staff meetings during the first few months of the year. Observe again during the last two months of the year, so that you can get a sense of changes over time. Try to take note of who speaks and how often. Listen also to the kinds of responses that various people get to their suggestions. As soon as you can, write your observations in your journal. Think about what your observations might tell you about decision-making, leadership and influence in the school. The following questions can help guide your observations. Some will be more easily answered during the latter part of the year than at the beginning.

- How do people talk about the meetings? Do they have a positive or negative attitude towards them?
- Who leads the meetings? Who attends the meetings? Are they mandatory or voluntary?
- Is there a set agenda? How is it developed?
- Is discussion encouraged or is the focus of the meeting the presentation of information? Who speaks? Who responds? What kinds of responses are given?
- Are committees formed? For what purposes? Is membership voluntary or mandated?
- What is the reaction to being on committees? Do the committees give reports at meetings?
- What happens when reports are given and committees make recommendations? Does it seem that plans are

made for acting on recommendations?
- Do people pay attention and seem involved, or are they engaged in unrelated activities while the meeting is going on?

You'll benefit from understanding not only who makes decisions and how they are made, but also how people feel about both the process and the decisions themselves. If teachers feel their opinions are heard and respected, they're likely to work together and to take more responsibility for implementing policies and decisions. As a new teacher, you'll more easily find support in such a school. If teachers feel that their voices aren't being heard, they're more likely to work in isolation and possibly even to rebel, to do what they want in their own classrooms, behind the safety of the closed door. You might have a difficult time getting information and help in this kind of school.

The decision-making process can affect not only the actual work and teaching that gets done, but also the social and psychological environment that exists. Isolation and disempowerment tends to breed suspicion and defensiveness. Empowerment and involvement in decision-making tends to encourage collaboration and trust.

Susan Moore Johnson's (1990) study of various schools found:

> The exercise of informal influence at all levels depended on the presence of responsive administrators and good personal relationships. . . . The emphasis on personal relationships suggests that it is commonly the well-positioned individual rather than the expert professional who successfully influences the decisions of the powers that be. (p.200)

It is to your advantage to find out who those "well-positioned individuals" are in your school. Not only might they be helpful to approach with your ideas, but they also might be able to fill you in on what's really going on in the school. On the other hand, because of their relationship with the "powers that be," you can't assume it is a good idea to confide in them.

At some schools, teachers will be ostracized if they get involved in decision-making roles. There may be a we-they mentality between teachers and administrators that discourages teachers from participation in what may be considered administrative decisions. Are teachers willing to participate in opportunities for decision-making? Are there "norms for equity" that discourage individual teachers from stepping forth and taking the lead (Johnson, 201)? Is there an unspoken norm that if you step forth and take a role in decision-making, you are a traitor to your colleagues?

You'll want to determine how different types of decisions are made, what structures there are, such as committees or school councils, and who is involved in the decision-making process. Also, learning about people's perceptions of decision-making will be interesting. Observing the processes of decision-making or governance tells you a great deal about the politics of the school.

2.4 Exercise for Your Journal: How are Decisions Really Made?

Try to find out who influences decisions in your school and how their involvement is perceived by others. During your second month in the school, talk about this to several of your colleagues; listen at meetings, in the Teachers' Room, and to casual conversations and remarks. Keep the following questions in mind and record your findings in a special section in your journal.

- How do people react to colleagues who express opinions at meetings?
- Do structures exist to involve teachers in decision-making? Do teachers want to participate?
- Who else participates in these structures (parents, students, other staff)? Do different people seem to be involved or is it the same few people all the time?
- Are there departments, teams, or clusters that make decisions? What kinds?
- Are decisions and policies actually implemented? Under what circumstances do policies seem to get implemented and when don't they?
- If you have an idea or a complaint about something, what can you do about it? To whom can you go? What happens when someone questions policy?
- How do colleagues talk about decisions that have been made? Do they feel included or not? Do they talk about why they feel this way?
- Who seems to have the closest relationship with the administration? How do you know? How are these people viewed by others?
- Do certain people seem to have more influence than others on decision-making? Who are they and why do

you think they have this influence?
- Are teachers involved in hiring decisions? Are parents involved in hiring decisions?
- Does the administrator/principal of your school have an open door policy? Do teachers, parents, and students seem to feel comfortable going into her office?

BACKGROUND OF YOUR COLLEAGUES

Workers care about the kinds of people they work with and for. Gender, race, ethnic background, and socioeconomic status all influence how workers experience their jobs and what they do in them. (Johnson, p. 15)

As you get to know your school and the people who work in it, try to learn about who they are as individuals. You'll better understand your colleagues if you think about their range of ages, their career and life stages, the times at which they entered the profession, and the prevailing educational philosophies at those times. These factors, as well as their gender and life experiences, will affect their behavior and their interpretation of events. Their backgrounds will influence their reactions to innovation and to you as a new teacher, their motivation to develop professionally, their interest in collegiality, and the culture of the school as a whole (Fullan & Hargreaves, 1996). Be careful not to stereotype, however. For example, you may think of older teachers as being more traditional than younger teachers, who are recently out of school. You might well find though that there are more experienced teachers who are much more open to sharing and innovative ideas than the newer teacher, still struggling to define herself.

Taking the time to get to know your colleagues personally, in a nonintrusive way, will pay off. It will help you to understand the context of your school and will suggest the ways you should and shouldn't approach your colleagues. Some of this information can be gained easily and early. Some will take a long time to find out. We certainly don't recommend that you ask very personal questions. You don't want to encourage gossip or be viewed as a busybody. Just be warm, friendly, and open to listening to your colleagues, and you'll probably be able to get to know many of them.

If you're invited to go out with a group after school, it might be a good idea to go. You can learn a lot from conversations outside of school. By making friends, you can learn who's who in the school community. If you refuse invitations, you might be seen as a snob. If most people socialize after school, you'll probably want to be included. Be aware, however, of the reputation of the group who has invited you, and think about how your participation will affect the way in which you are viewed by others. The more inclusive the group, the better.

As you become a part of your school and get to know your colleagues, you'll find, as in any group, people with diverse backgrounds, perspectives, needs, and philosophies. You'll need to learn how to integrate your ideas with theirs in order to live harmoniously in the community and make the most of your experience, both personally and professionally.

**2.5 Exercise for Your Journal:
Getting to Know Your Colleagues**

During the first month or two at your new school, make it your business to try to get to know several of your colleagues — other teachers, adminstrators, secretaries, custodians, and anyone else who works there. Questions such as those that follow may help you to learn more about people. Some of these can be answered by observation. Others may involve asking questions. Be subtle; you're not interviewing people. We're merely suggesting that you make an effort to talk to others and that you be more aware of listening to what they say in natural conversations. Write in your journal what you've learned about the composition of the group, and note how you think it might affect their behavior, your own behavior, and their expectations of you. The following are some of the questions that might guide you in learning about your colleagues:

- What is the population of teachers like? (age, diversity, gender)
- What language groups and cultures are represented among staff and students?
- How do people dress? Formally, in shirts, ties, jackets, or dresses? Or informally, in slacks and jeans?
- What is their professional background? How long have they been teaching here? In other schools? Have

they had other careers?
- Do they have families of their own? Children? How old? Aging parents?
- Do they have life situations which necessitate leaving school early or make it difficult to come in at night?
- What kinds of interests and hobbies do they have?

COLLEGIALITY AND INTERACTIONS

My experience in schools and universities suggests that the nature of relationships between adults and adults, between youngsters and youngsters, and between adults and youngsters has much more to do with a school's quality and character and with the accomplishments of student and teacher alike than does anything else. (Barth, 1996, p.6-7)

Do the norms and values of the school reflect an ethos of collegiality, or is there a sense of isolation among teachers? Getting to know your colleagues and learning about their backgrounds will help you to learn about the norms in the school. Relationships among adults in schools may take many different forms. Sometimes these relationships resemble the parallel play often found among preschool children.

Two three-year-olds are busily engaged in opposite corners of a sand-box. One has a shovel and bucket; one has a rake and a hoe. At no time do they share each other's tools. Although in proximity and having much to offer one another, each works and plays pretty much in isolation. (Barth, 1996, p.6)

In a school where parallel play is the norm, you might see several teachers with classrooms along the same corridor. One might be teaching a poetry unit using the books she has in her classroom; another might also be teaching a poetry unit with his books and might be having his students do a poetry reading for parents; a third might have a child in her class who has a parent who is a poet coming in to read her poetry. At no time do the teachers share either their books, resources, or ideas about how to teach the poetry unit. In other schools where collegiality is typical, you will see teachers working together, planning interdisciplinary units, meeting in teams, observing each others' classes, talking about teaching practice. Does the behavior in your school resemble parallel play, or is it characterized by collegiality and sharing? Elsewhere in this book, we discuss different forms and models of collegiality. Here we present an exercise that will help you to understand some of the issues related to interactions, collegiality, and isolation in your school. For a more detailed discussion of collegiality and how you can think about it, look at Chapter Six.

2.6 Exercise for Your Journal: Life in the Teachers' Room

A good place to begin your study of the school is in the Teachers' Room. Bring your lunch into the Teachers' Room. Sit quietly and observe as you eat. Do this on several different days during the first two or three weeks. If possible, go into the room at other times during the day also. Repeat this observation at various intervals throughout the year to see if there are any changes. As you listen and watch, assess what the conversation and activity tells you about the school. After you sit in the Teachers' Room, record your observations in your journal. Think about the following questions:

- What is the physical setup of the room? Comfortable sofas and chairs? Tables and chairs? How is the space arranged?
- What is on the walls? Professional notices? Conference flyers? School policies and rules? Cartoons? Photographs? Personal notes? What else?
- Is there coffee in the room? Other communal refreshments?
- Who is in the room?
- Who is sitting where and with whom? Are people talking in pairs or in small groups? Is there one large group discussion?
- Are certain people (e.g., student teachers, staff, paraprofessionals) excluded from the Teachers' Room?
- Do teachers, administrators and other staff members come into the room?
- How long do people stay in the room?
- What are the topics of conversation? Personal issues? Professional topics? Teaching ideas? Specific students/families? Colleagues? Are they making negative,

positive, or judgmental comments about students,
families, colleagues, their jobs, or the school?

When you have had several opportunities to observe, reread your observations and think about what you can extrapolate from your notes about what this experience in the Teachers' Room suggests. What are the unwritten norms and values? Does the experience suggest people you would want to go to for advice? Who would you avoid? What are considered acceptable topics for discussion? What issues seem to be unacceptable? Can you tell if there is a spirit of collegiality? Is there evidence of factions in the school? Are teachers supportive of one another? Do teachers consider parents allies or adversaries? Is there an atmosphere of professionalism?

These are just a few of the issues that may be clarified by spending time in the Teachers' Room. You will probably have many more insights. Of course, the information you have gained from these observations must be considered in the context of your experiences in the larger school. The Teachers' Room is merely one place to gain a window into what really goes on.

You should also be aware of some of these questions in the daily life of the school, in places other than the Teachers' Room. Your observations related to these questions will reveal the nature of the relationships among teachers and staff in your school. Thinking about your answers to these questions will help you to understand whether there is an atmosphere of collegiality and sharing among the teachers and administrators. After reflecting on these observations, you should be able to tell whom you can ask for help without fear of repercussions. You may also be able to tell who are the people who would be open to talking about ideas. As a new teacher, sharing of ideas and resources will be critical for your survival. You may have a better sense of whether you will need to look outside of the school for help and support, or whether you can get what you need among your colleagues. As a student teacher, your cooperating teacher should see her role as sharing ideas with you and giving you guidance. If you are a new teacher, you may have an assigned mentor. If there are other teachers in the school who are also willing to support you, your experience will even better prepare you for becoming a strong teacher. "Beginning teachers who enter a school culture in which the teachers share common goals and work collegially will likely enjoy a successful first year" (Brock & Grady, 1997, p.60).

FAMILIES AND COMMUNITY

Rather than seeing each other as adversaries vying for control of the education of a child, a teacher and a parent working in partnership can gain both personal and professional rewards that are unavailable when working in isolation. (Hulsebosch, 1992, chapter 7, p.111)

The relationship of families and other caregivers to the school is a critical aspect of understanding the culture of a school community. Although communication between home and school is an important ingredient in the success of children, the relationship between parents and teachers may be fraught with anxieties, misunderstandings, and lack of trust. As a new teacher, it will serve you well to learn about the community and family backgrounds of the children in your class. You also want to understand the norms related to involvement of, and attitudes toward, families in the school. Is the school welcoming to families? What efforts are made to involve families? What are the attitudes of teachers and administrators toward families or other caregivers? What is the attitude of families toward teachers and administrators? We will cover the issues related to families and community extensively in Chapters Four and Five. The following exercise will help you to become more sensitive to these aspects of your school. If possible, do it during the first couple of weeks in your school.

2.7 Exercise for Your Journal: Understanding the Community

There are many things you can do to gain an understanding of the community to which your school belongs. Try to discern what is valued, how people relate, the diversity of backgrounds represented. Try to do this in a nonjudgmental manner. The following are some suggestions of places you might go to learn more about the community of which your new school, and now you, are a part. Keep notes in your journal.

- Drive around the neighborhoods from which your students come. Don't just look at the neighborhood of the school. If school choice is involved in student assignment, then your students may live anywhere in the town or city in which the school is located. If possible, do this at different times of day and on weekends. Look at the housing, the people you see outside, level of activity, stores, and businesses.

- Stop at some neighborhood establishments, e.g., a grocery store, a pharmacy, a restaurant. If there are bulletin boards in any of these places, look at them. Take note of the kinds of activities on notices posted. What does this tell you about the interests and concerns of the community?
- Watch and listen to the people you see. How do they talk to each other? Especially notice how adults and children interact and how children interact with each other.
- If you see any students you know, how are you introduced to parents and what is said in your conversation?
- What appear to be the ethnic and linguistic backgrounds of the people in the community?
- Look at local newspapers. What kind of news is highlighted? What kind of community events are highlighted? What does all of this tell you about the community? Look especially for articles that relate to the schools.
- How many of the teachers in the school grew up or live in this community?
- What does everything you have observed, heard, and read tell you about the socieconomic backgrounds of people in the community? What does it tell you about the educational backgrounds of people in the community?

Think about how the information you have learned from this exercise can impact your work with the children (and other teachers) in the school. Given your understanding of the community, what might be some ways to involve the families of your students in the school/classroom? Are there particular experiences you might try to provide in order to reach the families more effectively? If many of the teachers in the school grew up or live in this community, how might you approach them to develop a relationship, in part, to have them help you understand the community? Think about your own attitude toward the people in the community. How can you uncover and examine any unconscious biases you might have? What can you do to change any negative attitudes?

SHARED TRADITIONS AND CULTURAL BONDS

Schools exist as distinct entities nestled within the context of a community and imbued with individual traditions, rituals, and shared stories and meanings. (Brock & Grady, 1997, p.52)

Some schools have strong cultural bonds and traditions that unite the school community. These might come from people having similar cultural or religious backgrounds or from being part of a stable neighborhood. These bonds may be most evident among the teaching staff, subsets of the community, or may even encompass the community as a whole. If the school is in a neighborhood where children walk home or are driven by parents, the cultural bonds may potentially encompass the whole community. Families may see one another at school, the playground, pool, place of worship, or local market and may feel connected because of the proximity of their homes as well as other commonalities that originally brought them to that community. In some school communities, you may even find that parents grew up in the neighborhood and attended the same schools as their children. Even if the area is not particularly stable, the potential for unity exists. Look for and take advantage of the commonalities in the community. Observe the elements of the cultural bonds and draw on them as resources for your formal and informal curriculum.

Many schools have traditions, such as annual events, fundraisers, rituals, celebrations, and ceremonies that are part of the fabric of the school community. These activities don't occur because of an interest of one teacher or parent. They can be counted on to happen throughout each school year, regardless of changes in staff and families. Find out about these traditions. You can incorporate into your curriculum class participation and real life planning related to these events. You can also base language projects and problem-solving activities on these school and community traditions and events as appropriate for your class.

If the bonds are evident among a subset of the community, find out what the differences are among the subsets and think about how to develop bridges to connect groups who could benefit from these extended cultural bonds. Seek to understand the possible conflicts or divisiveness that may exist between and among subgroups. How can you address issues through your curriculum that may strengthen the bonds that exist and extend these bonds to other subsets of the community? How can you minimize the damaging conflict that may influence children's classroom behavior? Try to help children develop friendships and relationships by learning about one another and simply working on meaningful group projects together.

If the bonds are most evident among the teaching staff only, use these cultural bonds to your advantage. Try not to be apprehensive about being an outsider, but be confident about joining this group which is bound by symbols and culture, and participate both in contributing to the needs of the community and meeting your own needs (Johnson, 1990). Sometimes you may feel somewhat intimidated by a cohesive faculty, especially if you are the only new hire for the year. Take your cues from the enthusiasm and excitement of the school community. You'll feel more in control when you incorporate tasks required for events and celebrations into your lessons and discussions in the classroom.

How might you determine whether or not there are strong cultural bonds in your school? The exercise on community in the previous section will help. After the next section on core values, you'll find another exercise which will help you understand the cultural bonds and traditions, as well as the core values in your school.

CORE VALUES

An organization has a core value if there is evidence of it everywhere:
   ❏ *it permeates the institution*
   ❏ *it drives the decisions*
   ❏ *it elicits strong reactions when it is violated*
   ❏ *and it's the very last thing you'll give up.* (Saphier, n.d.)

Many schools in the past few years have engaged in the process of developing core values. You may hear and see references to core values in your school. They may be written on banners, posters, and book-covers. Teachers and administrators may talk about them and may ask students to recite or discuss them. Even if schools haven't consciously gone through a formal process of articulating them, values and shared assumptions tend to exist in schools. Core values are, in a sense, the articulated, shared ideals of the entire school community. When a school community collaboratively develops four or five core values or outcomes for students, they are able to focus their energy and commitment in those areas that are considered important by all constituencies.

Developing core values has generally involved an extensive process of meetings, where values are prioritized and everyone in the community has an opportunity for input. After core values are chosen, they are stated as the concrete practices and behaviors that will be encouraged and expected by members of the school community. Children, parents, and teachers work together to plan ways to address the values in school and at home. Both the process and the product of developing core values are important. The discussions help to clarify expectations and can serve as a means of collaboration between staff and parents that is otherwise often missing in schools. Discussions about developing and implementing core values tend to occur extensively during the first year or so, while the core values are being determined. Later, various groups of people continue to revisit them, making sure that they are still relevant and being implemented. Some examples of core values that have been chosen by schools are:

> Students will acquire a strong academic foundation and an appreciation for the arts. They will join with teachers, family, and peers to create a learning environment that stimulates curiosity, creativity, and delight in the pursuit of knowledge. (Underwood School, Newton,MA, 1993)

> Students will gain respect for people's individual differences, valuing the contribution of each person. (Harvard Elementary School, Harvard, MA School Improvement Plan, 1995)

Both the core values themselves and the process by which they were developed will give you valuable insight into the community of your school. It will help you to understand how people work together, the degree of respect for varied opinions and constituencies, and the nature of what is valued.

2.8 Exercise for Your Journal:
Shared Traditions and Core Values

During the second month and then again around mid-year, spend some time walking around your school. Look carefully at the halls, classrooms, offices, and other spaces. As you observe, think about the messages that are conveyed by what you see on display. Also, listen to conversations that may give you clues about what is valued by the school community. Ideally, there will be a relationship between traditions of the school and the core values espoused. Record your observations and possible interpretations in your journal. The following questions can help guide your observations. If you keep some of these questions in mind at the beginning of the school year, and again as the year progresses, you'll begin to get a sense of what is important to people in the school. You'll also better understand what kind of behavior is expected.

- Are there school traditions or regularly occurring events in which staff, students, and/or families participate?
- Are there visible signs of these traditions (i.e., posters, artwork, newspaper clippings)?
- How do people talk about these traditions? Do you get a sense of excitement and enthusiasm or a sense of obligation, even dread?
- Do most people attend these traditional events?
- Do there seem to be common cultural bonds which unite large groups or subgroups of people in the school? What are they?
- Are core values articulated? What are they? See if you can find out how they were developed.
- Are the core values visible? Are they posted in the school? Do people talk about them? How? Is there a sense of seriousness and commitment when they are discussed, or a sense of cynicism?
- What kinds of displays are up on bulletin boards in the office? In the halls? In the Teachers' Room? Do these reflect the core values?
- Does the behavior of students, staff, and families reflect the core values?

- How are the core values reinforced?
- Is there a school newsletter? What kinds of articles are in it?
- What kinds of accomplishments of children are rewarded and shared? What kinds of accomplishments of staff are rewarded and shared? Are they consistent with the school's core values?

PROFESSIONAL DEVELOPMENT OPPORTUNITIES

> . . . *the professional development of teachers: engaging them in a wide variety of opportunities for growth in knowledge and skills within the education profession.* (Loucks-Horsley, Harding, Arbuckle, Murray, Dubea, & Williams, 1987, p.3).

Learning about professional development opportunities in your school and school system will give you another window into the culture of your school, and will help you understand how your own growth will be supported. Not only will it be important to find out how your school and the system handle professional development, but it will also be important to understand the attitudes of teachers and administrators towards the professional development offered. You can think about professional development as the ways in which teachers are offered, find, and create opportunities to continually learn more about the art and craft of teaching. Ideally, professional development should be woven into the fabric of teaching — integrated into the life and values of the school. In order for you and your colleagues to grow and change, to keep up with current educational ideas, to continue to be excited about your work, you need to take advantage of meaningful professional development opportunities.

You might find that you're working in a system where a wide range of opportunities are offered. Teachers and administrators encourage, support, and value professional development. Your colleagues may be excited about discussing workshops they've attended and eager to share what they've learned. Teachers are given time to participate in activities which advance the priorities of the school, as well as activities which help them to meet their own goals. School priorities are determined with the input of teachers, and you feel that your opinion is sought and valued. Teachers engage in classroom-based inquiry where they examine their teaching and share their findings and knowledge. Professional development in this kind of school is usually more than one-shot deals. People are nurtured over time to improve their practice. Everyone is encouraged to learn and grow; you feel that change and new ideas are welcome.

You may have heard about one example of this type of environment, the Professional Development School (PDS), which is a mutually beneficial long-term partnership between a school and a college. PDSs are dedicated to the preparation of preservice teachers, the professional development of teachers, the creation of knowledge about teaching practice through collegial reflection and inquiry, and the enhancement of learning for all children. Professional Development Schools are environments which are intentionally created to be communities of learning for adults and children. If you're working in such a school, you may have access to many exciting opportunities.

You may, like many teachers, however, work in a system where professional development opportunities are sporadic or nonexistent. You and your colleagues may feel that you are being forced to participate in meaningless activities, based entirely on the whims of upper level administrators who are perceived as out of touch with the real needs of the school. Teachers who seek out opportunities to advance their own learning are seen as working too much or "making the rest of us look bad." Many of the teachers want to keep everything the same and fear change. New ideas are viewed with suspicion. Teachers in such a school rarely discuss their teaching practice or other professional issues.

Your experience will vary significantly depending on what type of setting you are in. As a beginning teacher or a student teacher, you'll probably be perceived as bringing with you new ideas. In the first type of school, one where professional development thrives, your colleagues will want to hear those ideas. You can expect that they will support you in your own learning and will probably want to discuss ideas about teaching. You may have a mentor, who will, in a sense, provide you with individualized professional development. You may have the chance to participate in a variety of experiences, such as attending workshops and conferences; working in your classroom with consultants; planning, meeting, and team-teaching with colleagues; speaking in college classes; working with practicum students and university faculty; participating in study groups; or getting feedback from your colleagues.

In the second type of setting, where professional development is a low priority, your opportunities, both formal and informal, for learning within the school may be quite restricted. If you talk about your ideas or say anything that might be seen as questioning or critical, you may be perceived as a know-it-all. You may hear patronizing phrases like "just wait until you see what the real world is like," or "when I was your age, I was idealistic too." You may come to feel that your school is not a safe place in which to discuss your ideas about teaching, and you may have difficulty finding opportunities to learn from your colleagues or from others who come into the school. You may find it necessary to create your own professional development opportunities through such avenues as professional organizations and networks or college courses. See Chapters Six and Nine for a more thorough discussion of ways to sustain yourself and grow professionally. A negative professional development environment will leave you feeling tired and resentful. A positive professional development situation makes you feel energized and excited. Even if you start out exhausted, involvement in good professional development rejuvenates you.

Assessing the climate and opportunities for professional development within your school will help you to see what is available, to figure out if you need to go elsewhere for learning, and to determine how you might behave with your colleagues. As a beginning teacher, you want to share with colleagues, you want to grow, and you want to continue the process of becoming a lifelong learner. The questions which follow will help you to look as those aspects of your school which are related to professional development. Paying attention to issues discussed in the sections of this chapter on collegiality and on external partnerships will also give you some ideas about professional development opportunities available at your school.

2.9 Exercise for Your Journal: Professional Development

In order to understand professional development at your school, read flyers and notices on bulletin boards, listen to announcements, talk to teachers and administrators. Try to find out the answers to as many of the following questions as possible. Keep a section of your journal on professional development opportunities and make notes in it throughout the year.

- Are there professional development opportunities offered? Do people take advantage of them? Who and how many? How are they advertised?
- Are workshops mandatory? Who plans them? Who presents at them?
- Are there other kinds of professional development endeavors in the school and/or the district? Describe. Is there ongoing work to help support learning and change, or are most activities one-shot deals?
- How do people talk about the professional development experiences? Do they see them as valuable? Or a waste of time?
- Is there any evaluation of professional development activities?
- Is time set aside for professional development? How much? Early release days? Whole days?
- Do teachers write professional development plans and set goals for themselves? How are these plans implemented?
- Does the administration support professional development? Do they participate?
- Who plans professional development? Are teachers asked for their input? What is the structure for planning and getting input?
- Do teachers share expertise with colleagues, or are outside "experts" generally brought in?
- Is this a Professional Development School? Are there Professional Development Schools in the system?
- Are there other kinds of partnerships with colleges or other agencies or organizations?
- Is there a mentoring program for new teachers? Describe.
- Are mentors given time or stipends?
- Is there another type of program for supporting beginning teachers? Describe.
- Is there an orientation program for new teachers? What kinds of things are included? Who facilitates it?
- Is tuition reimbursement offered for teachers who want to take college courses?
- Are teachers funded and/or given time to attend conferences? Do teachers present papers at conferences?
- Do teachers come in to school early? Stay late? What are

they doing during these times?
• Is there encouragement and support to engage in classroom inquiry? (see Chapter Seven)

EXTERNAL PARTNERSHIPS

Successful partnerships are characterized by an exchange of ideas, knowledge and resources. Partners form a mutually rewarding relationship to improve some aspect of education, and the relationship must be based on the identification and acceptance of compatible goals and strategies. In addition, the partners should respect the differences in each other's culture and style, striving to apply the best of both worlds to achieve established goals. (OERI, 1993, as cited in Danzberger, Bodinger-deUriarte, & Clark, 1996, p. 1)

Schools have varied relationships with community agencies, such as colleges, human service agencies, and businesses. Access to these external entities can provide a valuable resource for the school and for you as a teacher. These relationships can serve as a source of human resources, such as student teachers and volunteer help in the classroom or in the school; they can provide financial resources, such as donations or assistance in fund-raising and grant-writing activities; they can offer opportunities for professional development, such as consultants from colleges. Partnerships with community agencies can also facilitate obtaining needed services for students. Such services as before or after school programs, health care, counseling, and parenting assistance can be more easily provided when positive relationships with outside agencies exist.

The extent to which partnerships are developed can be an indication of the openness of the school. A school that encourages partnerships must have a degree of comfort with having people observing activities. Partnerships with colleges, for example, imply a willingness to accept student teachers and/or to work with college faculty. These types of relationships help to enhance the professional development of teachers in a school. If a school is genuinely engaged in such partnerships, you might infer that there's a commitment to professional development.

2.10 Exercise for Your Journal: Finding Out About Partnerships

Make it your business to learn what partnerships exist and what their purposes and activities are. Over the course of the year, as you learn about partnerships, make notes in a special section of your journal. Think about how the resources available might help you and your class. You might consider the following questions:

- What organizations, agencies, colleges, and businesses have a connection to your school?
- How are the partnerships defined? Are they formal or informal? A long term commitment or for a specific purpose? What are the goals — stated and unstated?
- Who is involved in the activities of the partnership? What do they do?
- What do people think of the partnerships?
- How do they seem to benefit your school? The other organizations involved?

Find out who are the people who are most involved in partnership activities and get to know them; they could be people who are willing to share ideas. They might also be aware of resources that will help you in your quest to become the best teacher you can be.

SUMMARY

The features discussed in this chapter will give you an introduction to understanding the major elements that make up the culture of a school. Hopefully, we've also helped you to see why it's important to know the culture. Now that you have begun studying your school, what do you do with the information? Start by thinking carefully about what you've learned. Are there are certain people you would want to approach with different kinds of questions or for specific types of advice? Are there some people you might want to avoid? You'll find that you are better able to avoid the sense of "going it alone" by connecting with teachers you feel will be supportive. Your analysis of the setting may influence any decisions you make regarding participation.

Understanding the nature of the school culture and learning how to work best within it should ultimately help you become a more effective teacher, find support from others, and become a part of the school. It's important to understand where the resources are and how to access them, the people whom you should or shouldn't approach for various kinds of help, the interpersonal dynamics in the school, and the general nature of the surrounding community. If you are aware of these aspects of your school, as well as of expectations, both stated and unstated, you will fare much better than if you remain naive.

We realize that you won't walk into your new school and immediately begin an assessment like this. As we said at the beginning of this chapter, it may take quite a while to figure out the various aspects of the culture, but it will be valuable for you to do so. Your ability to function effectively as a professional will be impacted by your knowledge of your school. Your understanding of your school as a workplace and as a learning environment will help you to figure out how you can fit in, learn what you need to, and maintain your values and ideals.

Suggested Resources

Barth, R.S. (1990). *Improving schools from within.* San Francisco: Jossey-Bass.

Beyond instructional leadership (2002). *Educational Leadership, 59* (8).

Johnson, S.M.(1990). *Teachers at work: Achieving success in our schools.* New York: Basic Books.

Lieberman, A. & Miller, L. (1992). *Teachers: Their world and their work.* New York: Teachers College Press.

Sarason, S. (1996). *Revisiting "The culture of the school and the problem of change."* New York: Teachers College Press.

CHAPTER THREE

GETTING TO KNOW
YOUR STUDENTS

Seeing the student first and then creating the environment — these challenges are the foundation for becoming an excellent teacher. (Ayers, 1995, p. 8)

You have a huge influence on the culture of your classroom. Remember that your students, who will likely be quite different every year, have an influence too. From their stories, pictures, original plays, songs, journals, raps, and dances throughout the year, you will get a sense of who these people are in your room. Using this information and academic assessments, you can strive to develop a comprehensive curriculum and create a culture of success for all. Your class will have a high level of trust and optimism when you treat students as individuals and capitalize on their positive influence on the classroom culture. Your students may show different aspects of their personalities depending on where they are: in your classroom, another classroom, the hallways and playgrounds, or at home. Learn as much as you can about who they are in these different contexts. Your goal is to become acquainted with the whole child.

On the first day, some students will stand out from the group because of characteristics that you won't ever forget (even if you try!). Work at getting to know more about these students. Set goals for yourself for the first day, first week, and first month to get acquainted. Develop a contract with yourself to know all the children well by the night of the school's Open House, which is usually four or five weeks after school starts. Be systematic about getting to know the students in your class. Include this process in your daily plans and check yourself often. By the time you meet parents and families, you can be assured that you are on your way to a successful year. Once they see how well you know their children, they will be more likely to share their sense of their child as well as their goals and aspirations with you. They will become partners with you in the educational process.

Getting to know your students communicates that you are interested in them as individuals. Students will appreciate your efforts to get to know them. They will more easily develop a trust in you. You can become a friend, mentor, and role model. You are showing your commitment to help them grow and develop. Use their ideas and interests to develop a learning community in your classroom. Include them in planning and give them choices about how to approach their learning.

Formal and informal assessment and observation will help you to determine the needs of the whole class, small groups, and individuals. Plan the first days and weeks of school to be primarily activities where you can observe the learning styles, intelligences, and temperament of students in your class. Begin by designing a variety of learning activities that will meet the varying needs of students. Ages and abilities will most likely vary by more than a year at any single grade level. You can use published inventories for math and reading to group youngsters if you choose to have groups for those subjects. You can use various writing and communication exercises to evaluate grammar, spelling, and language development while getting students to write about topics that help you get to know more about them and what they like.

BUILDING A COMMUNITY IN YOUR CLASSROOM

Before School Starts

You can begin to get acquainted with your students before school starts. Write a postcard to each student introducing yourself and commenting about how excited you are about the beginning of school. "Dear Keisha, My name is Ms. Jackson, and I am your third grade teacher. I look forward to meeting you on the first day of school. I have a surprise for you." The surprise can be a new pencil, a fun-shaped eraser, or a special poem you have written for the class. You may want to write to parents also. Keep your letter short and simple. If you need to do so, get it translated into the languages of your students' families. Mail these so they arrive a few days before school starts.

Strategies for the First Day

Learn your students' names on the first day in a self-contained class-

room or the first few days if you have several departmentalized classes. Use a seating chart to record names and have the students make
name tags to wear or put on their desks. Observe your students' interactions with one another. You can discover on the first day those who
are extremely quiet, extremely loud, and those who are aggressive or
assertive. We suggest that you write down your impressions, but caution you to write them in pencil. You may be wrong about that child,
and children, like all people, change. Be careful not to pigeonhole students and make sure you reexamine any negative impressions you
have. Figure out how you can be instrumental in getting positive
results for each student.

The Best First Day of School Ever!

You may be fortunate enough to have several weeks to plan your first
day, or you may have only a few days. Regardless of when you find out
what grade you will be teaching, you can begin preparation well ahead
of the big day. Find out how to obtain materials that are provided by
your school such as posterboard, markers, scissors, glue and construction paper. You may want to purchase other kinds of colorful paper,
borders for your bulletin board, and 3"x5" cards and a file or a journal
for your notes. Think about the activities that you want to do, and
double check to be sure you have all the materials in hand. Prepare
extra copies and extra sets of materials in case of a mishap or in case
you have several more students than are on your class list. Actually
doing the activities yourself will help you know what materials are
needed and how long an activity takes. You will discover how much
glue is too much to work well, which markers do not show up on which
colors or textures of paper. Talk with other teachers about what you
intend to do, and get their feedback and warnings regarding any pit-
falls you might anticipate. You will need to have some activities that
youngsters can do with little supervision, as you will inevitably experience distractions and interruptions throughout the day. In three
words, our advice is to *plan, plan, plan*. Write down your best guess
for a schedule in 15 or 20 minute modules. Remember to check on specialists' lunch and playground schedules, which are usually not flexible. You can assign the rest of the time any way you want.

   You will be excited and nervous about the first day of school and so
will your students and their families. What are some things you could
do for the first day in fourth grade, for example? Plan a low key day
with lots of opportunities for you and your students to get acquainted

and feel success. Expect parents to come in and say hello (and look you over) if they are dropping off students themselves. Put out games, puzzles, and activities at a variety of ability levels for the first students so that they can occupy themselves while everyone else is arriving. Let students make their own name tags to wear or put on their desks. Have samples of those you have made with your name completed. Remember that the students in your class will have a variety of interests, abilities, and possibly even ages.

Play a name learning game as soon as everyone has arrived. Sit on the floor in a circle and start by giving your name and something you like (real or imagined) that starts with the same sound as your name. I am Ms. Jones and I like Jell-O. Each child repeats all the ones before her and adds herself and some favorite item. Encourage students to help each other if needed. When the circle is finished, it's up to you to recite every name and what they like. You will amaze yourself at how well you can do after the repetition in the form of a game. A little reinforcement with name tags as reminders should get you to the end of the day knowing everybody's name.

On the first day, include a wide range of activities that speak to different strengths, talents, and interests. You may want to have students:

- ❏ write a story
- ❏ draw a picture
- ❏ do some mathematics review including a few challenging problems
- ❏ create a role-play about their summer
- ❏ read a story out loud
- ❏ read a story silently and talk about it
- ❏ write their first journal entry about their day
- ❏ make up a song or rap
- ❏ sing a song
- ❏ make rubbings or a collage with leaves, seeds and weeds
- ❏ recite some poetry together
- ❏ perform a dance
- ❏ listen to music

Assume you will get a late start. Throw in snack, lunch, recess and the next thing you know, the day is over! Before it is time to go, stop to review with the students what they learned today so when their parents ask them later at home what they did at school, they won't say "nothing!" Give out the surprises you promised in your post card.

Relax for a few minutes; then start working out the details for tomorrow!

Activities for the First Week

During the first week, talk with each student individually each day. Always say something positive to each student daily. During the week, ask about their thoughts, feelings, and opinions regarding school. Find out what they like about school and what they dislike. Get them to talk about last year, especially what they felt good about accomplishing. Ask older students about a favorite teacher and why they liked him or her. Keep notes, especially during the first few weeks of school. Use separate 3"x5" cards for each student and file them regularly or use your journal. Do as much detailed planning as you can for the whole week to minimize daily stress.

Here are some sample questions to use with your students. You can ask them orally as part of a discussion or as a written survey, but don't use them all at once.

- ❏ What do you like best about school?
- ❏ What do you like least about school?
- ❏ What would you change if you could make changes in the school day?
- ❏ What do you think you will learn this year?
- ❏ What would you like to work on most this year?
- ❏ What was your best subject last year?
- ❏ What do you remember most about last year?
- ❏ Who is your favorite teacher ever and why?
- ❏ Would you go back to see that teacher and talk to him or her if you could? What would you say?
- ❏ As an optional activity, students could write a letter to that teacher.

Does each student feel he or she is really good at some school-related subject or activity? In most instances you will have to make it a priority to help a student uncover gifts and talents. Your academic assessments will be helpful in this area. However, don't limit your scope to reading and math, neglecting other areas of the curriculum. You may not immediately feel a need to attend to music or art skills, but these areas may be the only way some of your students can excel at school.

Consider performing arts or martial arts as ways for students to be stars. Some may be excellent soccer players, dancers, or swimmers. Assessing their skills and integrating their interests into the classroom core are daunting tasks that mean significant investment on your part. Skilled, experienced teachers seem to do this kind of assessment intuitively. As a new teacher you can start with the obvious curricular areas and branch out to others as best you can. The strategies suggested throughout this chapter are a beginning. What is most important is to be aware that your room is full of talented students, and you can discover and celebrate those talents in each of the students.

Language arts activities should go beyond the usual "what I did for summer vacation." Use a series of assignments to have students write stories of all kinds. These will tell you something about the author. Give them a chance to draw pictures and write a song, poem, or a rap. Other ways of communicating their ideas besides writing or drawing include making audio tapes, videotapes, creating a collage, or acting out scenes with other students.

Notice during the first days who is eager with hands always up to ask questions, answer questions, or make comments. Who is the child that shrinks back, obviously afraid to be called on? Is the behavior noticeable all day or during certain periods such as math or reading? These behaviors communicate something to you. You should try to figure out what they mean. It may indicate that a child is an introvert or extrovert. It may indicate that the child is math phobic or is sensitive because he or she isn't as good at reading aloud as some classmates. It may also indicate that someone is not having a good day.

Acknowledge and celebrate the unique talents of each student. One way to do this is by having a student of the day or the week as a part of your lessons. Choose a student each week to have a designated show and tell time to bring family photos, memorabilia, and scrapbook items to share with the class. Since this will take most of the year for each class member to have a whole week, you might want to choose those students you don't know well to present during the first few months. Think of featuring two students a week.

Activity 3.1 Student of the Week

This Student of the Week activity, suggested by a beginning third grade teacher, can be an excellent integrated lesson:

Send a note home the first week of school introducing parents and families to the idea. Make some suggestions about the kinds of things students can bring in, such as photos of themselves, photos of special events, trips to visit grandparents, vacations, or camp. Students can draw pictures if they don't have photos to use.

Give each child a posterboard and rubber cement to mount the photos a week ahead of time. Be mindful that the posterboard is not bigger than the student who is carrying it home! The rubber cement allows you to remove the photos later without damage. They can write a few words under each photo to help them remember the significance. They can bring in sample items from a collection or a momento that is special to their culture, religion, or ethnicity. They can also bring in favorite items that aren't nec-essarily part of a collection. Post the pictures on a prominent bul-letin board with appropriate headings.

Select or engage the students in developing the schedule to take turns for student of the week. This can be a good problem-solv-ing activity. Some choices would be to have students do this on or near birthdays, have them draw from a hat, or go in alphabetical order. Some students think being first is always best. This is a good time to discuss the pluses and minuses of being at the very beginning or very end. For example, those who are last will have more time to prepare, and they can get ideas and learn from the way others present.

On a designated day of the week, have the student introduce her-self or himself and show special items related to significant events in life. Allow the class to ask questions for clarification and more information. The student can manage the group discussion alone or with your help and choose from those who indicate they have questions. After the interview, ask students to write or draw about the honored student as a language or communication activity.

You can also set aside time for others to make positive comments and compliments about the student in morning meeting or circle time. If your classes are departmentalized, you can spend a few minutes each day with this simple activity instead of student of the week. Classmates can mention anything they like about the selected student. This activity increases self-esteem and builds community so you will all know one another a little better. In addition, you will be filling your storehouse of knowledge of the students in your classroom.

Remember, do as much detailed planning as you can for the whole week to minimize your daily stress. Try to stay as far ahead of upcoming days as you can. Even though you may have to revise your plans, based on the progress your students have made, you will feel more confident knowing your direction.

Strategies for the First Month

One strategy to include students in planning is to use Ogle's (1986) KWL charts to enlist their input for a new unit of study. Ogle has suggested the following:

1. Use large sheets of chart paper or poster board divided into three vertical columns.

2. Start with a list of what the students tell you they already know (K) about the topic to be studied. This first step is a welcome positive experience for many students who need you to acknowledge the skills and concepts they have mastered and validate their strengths. If you are going to study Latin American countries, students can tell you what they know about the people, customs, and geography, for example.

3. Next, find out what they want (W) to learn about the topic. What are they curious about? Then create the second column of the list with their answers to these questions. They may want to learn about the games children play in other countries or the type of music or dance that is popular now or historically. You can easily gather this information in a whole class discussion orally.

4. Leave space in the third column for them to list what they

learn (L) during their studies and at the culmination of a unit. Finally, post these lists in a prominent place in the room for all to see. Use their questions to guide your planning along with guidance from standards from national and local curricula.

This process is very useful as one of your assessment tools, as well as an empowering experience for the students in your class.

The KWL chart will help you to make it a priority to give students what they need, both academically and personally. If you have this posted at Open House, you can use it to communicate with parents and families about the work you are doing in the class, the progress you have made, and the plans for future study.

Understanding your students' prior knowledge will allow you to build your curriculum starting with whatever students can do well. If you begin this way, they will be interested and motivated, anticipating success for the coming year. Vary your curriculum content, activities, and mode of assessment to reflect the diverse needs of the students. Classrooms tend to be too focused on the three "R's" with student writing and teacher talk. Integrate literature, science, social studies, art, and music in your offerings. Integration of these subjects makes learning more interesting and teaches skills and concepts in ways more sensible to students. They can transfer their learning more easily and remember more for those standardized tests they are inevitably required to take. Active involvement is key to all learning, regardless of age or grade level. Be creative about keeping youngsters at the center of learning. Plan for them to work in small groups with hands-on activities, or individually on projects that facilitate movement about the room. Involve them in discussing respectful behavior during those times, and be clear about agreed upon guidelines.

Every teacher appreciates the quick learner, the polite, cooperative child, and the motivated learner. What about the rest? Assume every student in your room can be motivated, can be cooperative, and take a closer look at the child who struggles. Sometimes it may be a youngster's persistence that is to be supported and admired. This student sticks with the task to the finish line even if he finishes last. Spotlight the valuable lesson that others can learn from that child. Look for and validate other non-traditional talents. Many schools value those who are smartest in traditional ways: fastest at reading, reading the most books, and first to finish in math or memorize the most basic facts. As you learn more about the students in your room, you may discover one who is an excellent gymnast, musician, peacemaker, or thinker. That's something to share with parents as you talk about their child in the class at Open House and at conferences.

Many successful teachers create what they refer to as a learning community in their classroom. This community provides a safe atmosphere for students to take risks, make mistakes, and learn from those mistakes. The students need to feel safe with you and the others in the room. Begin your community development early and continue throughout the school year (Halaby, 2000).

3.1 Exercise for Your Journal: Two Strategies for Building a Learning Community

Try these two strategies during the first month and write your reflections in your journal.

Building Community with the In-Common Quilt Lesson

This is an interdisciplinary lesson which touches on skills and concepts in several school subjects. The quilt is a grid that students use to record the ways they are alike and the ways they are different from one another. Veteran teachers recommend this activity to help build community in the classroom. For a beginning of school activity, divide the class into groups of four or five and explain that they will create a quilt depicting one thing they like or dislike that makes them different from the group and two they share with each person in the group. List these on the grid given in class.

Before the lesson, draw a grid with four or five rows and columns. Write student names across the top and down the left in the same order. Use large sheets of newsprint with colorful markers or crayons. Give the students the papers after giving them instructions for developing the quilts, and assign work spaces for group work. When they finish their quilts, ask students to share the discoveries about their classmates and themselves.

The activity relates to several of Gardner's (1983) multiple intelligences, which are discussed later on in the chapter. The activity requires discussion, reflection, writing, or drawing; these represent the linguistic, logical-mathematical, spatial, interpersonal, and intrapersonal intelligences.

Building Community with a Multiple Intelligences Lesson

Thomas Armstrong (2000) discusses the multiple intelligences hunt as a unique treasure hunt. In this activity you can give students a list of tasks which represent each of Gardner's eight intelligences. They have to find someone in the class who can complete the task. Older students enjoy actually creating their own list as a part of the lesson if there is sufficient time. The possibilities are endless. Here are a few, representing each intelligence (cited in parentheses).

- hum or sing a few lines (musical)
- recite a poem (linguistic)
- share an imaginary experience (intrapersonal)
- count by sixes (logico-mathematical)
- skip around the room (bodily-kinesthetic)
- sketch one area of the room (spatial)
- identify a tree from leaves, or seeds (naturalistic)
- do this exercise with students from another class (interpersonal)

You can get to know the students through this activity as well as introduce them to multiple intelligences. You may surprise their parents at Open House with the talents you have discovered in their children.

ASSESSING THE ACADEMICS

A major activity by the end of the first two months of school is the Open House when parents meet their child's teacher, followed closely by their first conferences. The parents are interested in meeting and getting some first impressions of the new teacher. This first meeting can be particularly important for your subsequent relationship with the children's families. Therefore, you want to be knowledgeable about each student in your class.

All parents want to know your impressions of their child's academic performance and any teaching plans you may have developed. Clearly, the impressions that give a sense of each student can be derived from your contacts with the child as you have worked with her in the classroom and with formal and informal measures. Hence, getting to know each student should start with assessing her academic skills. Find out what students already know about the content of all the subjects you are teaching. Consider what students have already learned, their abilities, and their motivations. Students whose abilities are several grades above or below grade level will require adapted materials.

All school districts require certain kinds of assessments. Standardized tests are administered at the same time of year, usually once a year. Test scores and percentiles are designed to compare students at a particular grade level. Some school systems require other kinds of assessments, with schoolwide grading and reporting procedures. You should become acquainted with these procedures and how they are used. Supplement those required assessments with your own assessment such as interviewing, questioning (oral or written), and observation. Consider using manipulative materials to compare students' performance with the more usual paper and pencil test materials. Consult with your grade level team or other colleagues to see what types of assessments they are planning. Your textbook series usually has built-in assessments that serve as benchmarks connected with specific grade levels. Acquaint yourself with existing materials before creating your own.

Cognitive assessment can be used to get to know your students academically. The results of this assessment can assist in planning your lessons for the class. These results can also be used to group students together to work on a specific skill or concept, or can provide feedback about the teaching/learning process throughout the year. When determining the cognitive level for math or reading, select several measures and look at the aggregate of the information you gather. Sometimes several measures will reveal the same strengths and weaknesses. At other times, your results may be contradictory. Many factors influence the information you get, including your own subjectivity, the way a child feels at the time you do the inventory, and the validity of the measure you are using. Even the published inventories have a margin of error, so don't put too much stock into any one assessment alone. You will have access to narratives from past teachers in cumulative folders and standardized test scores as a reference when planning for youngsters individually.

Other kinds of assessment data you may consider include standardized achievement tests such as the Stanford 9 or Metropolitan

Achievement Test. These tests generate scores, percentiles, and grade level information for individuals, usually with separate subtest scores in math, reading, and language skills. The child's record will likely contain achievement test scores, as well as scores derived from the diagnostic instruments that accompany the textbook series and teacher-made diagnostic tests.

Another type of assessment is the use of portfolios. You can create portfolios by collecting each student's work, including individual items such as self-assessments, work samples, and writing samples. One way to use the portfolios is to have students compile their work throughout the year and reflect on their work samples. At times like parent conferences, for example, they might reflect orally or in writing on the significance of the particular pieces they've selected.

Design pre-tests based on reading or math concepts and skills you believe to be appropriate for the students in your class and for what you will teach. List the objectives from your district curriculum or grade level textbooks, then develop two or three items for each of the objectives. Although this may seem like a rough measure, it is useful combined with other measures you may use. Good sources of objectives in addition to your basic texts and district curriculum are state and national standards. These will give you broad guidelines regarding the sequence of skill development and expectations for your grade level. If you are a student teacher beginning in a spring semester, consult with your cooperating teacher about the strategies for the development of the classroom routine and the initial student assessment which was used in September. You will still need to acquaint yourself with students and the classroom climate in general.

While the measures we have suggested are heavily weighted toward elementary students, the formal and informal measures for reading and math will be similar across grade levels, though the actual skills vary as will the difficulty levels.

Reading Assessment

Paradoxically, the connection between assessment of a skill and the kinds of instruction offered is a relatively recent practice. Reading assessment is often connected to teaching students because the ability to read is important and reading proficiency is integrally related to learning content. A network of skills have been identified that facilitate or inhibit reading proficiency.

Reading assessment involves assessing two different kinds of skills:

the mechanics, the skills on which reading is based, e.g., letter recognition, and letter sounds, and reading in the global sense, i.e., extracting meaning from the text. These two types of skills require different kinds of teaching techniques and different types of assessment. That is, mechanics are taught at the lower grades predominantly as the mechanics are mastered. Reading for meaning is the predominant focus in the higher grades, although one is concerned with meaning even before he starts reading.

A common and longstanding approach to assessing a child's reading is to have her read paragraphs aloud that are graded for difficulty, recording the errors the child makes as she reads the selection, how long it takes her to read it, and the fluency with which she reads. The classical test is Gray's Oral Reading Paragraphs. With older students, the selections are longer. Also, the concerns expand to include reading for meaning (comprehension) and analysis of the underlying story and its implications.

A less satisfactory but more convenient measure for setting grade level performance uses graded word lists. The basal level is established when the child reads words of increasing difficulty with no errors; when he reads words successively, making mistakes with each one, he has reached his ceiling level. His active zone for reading is between these two levels.

Skills that benefit from direct teaching can be assessed through a strategy of testing directly to the instruction for the skill. In a dynamic manner, you can develop short tests for tasks such as letter recognition or comprehension by selecting items and presenting them to students as they have progressed through a series of lessons. To develop a test, write the items from easy to hard, to see whether the students have acquired the skill you have been teaching. At set points in the series of lessons you completed, students solve the test items. This type of cycle enables you to check their learning and enables you to check whether your teaching is accomplishing your goals. You will learn the rate and how well each student learns. This strategy of connecting instruction to assessment can be applied throughout the school year. Formal tests can provide corroboration of students' progress.

You can derive useful individualized test scores to share with parents by using reading inventories. Reading inventories are included as part of most basal reading programs, can be purchased separately, or can be teacher-developed. Inventories provide an entry reading level for each child, using oral reading passages or graded word lists. The student works with these stimuli until he makes a certain number of errors, indicating when he reaches beyond his level. The score levels indicate the passage corresponding to his reading level.

A sample reading inventory, the Ekwall/Shanker (1999), allows you to choose the kind of assessment of reading skills you want to complete while getting to know your students. Among the tests in this battery, you will find oral reading, reading comprehension, basic sight vocabulary, and phonemic awareness. If this resource is available through your school, use it. What you may want to select first is a quick screening device to guide your initial classroom instruction. You can expect to have student abilities vary both above grade level and below. The Ekwall/Shanker offers passages based on widely accepted readability formulas and a Graded Word List (GWL). The quick assessment or GWL can be used to guide you to the passages to choose for each student. Once you determine the student's reading level, you can choose appropriate materials for instruction and help students in making appropriate selections for independent reading.

Another frequently used form of assessment is running records (Clay, 1993). Teachers use a separate sheet to record the miscues and score the types of mistakes made while a student is reading aloud. An analysis of the miscues helps teachers determine types of strategies each child is using to read. Using running records may be challenging at first, but gets easier with experience.

A test for assessing phonemic awareness in young children by Hallie Yopp (1986) was published in *The Reading Teacher*. This inventory is useful in the primary grades to help you get to know your students' ease with hearing and manipulating sounds. It is very user-friendly and can be administered and scored in minutes.

If you do not have access to graded passages for reading, or a published inventory, try the following practices of experienced teacher.

Select a book from the reading materials available in your room:

- ask each of your students to read aloud to you from the text.
- spend a few minutes following along and listening to assess how well the student decodes.
- observe whether the reading is fluent, whether the student points at or reads one word at a time without expression, or whether the student uses a monotone or accurate response to punctuation.
- observe whether the student displays anxiety during the task.

Johnson and Kress (1997) have listed certain behavioral characteristics commonly observed in students at their independent, instructional, and frustration reading levels. Some of these related behavioral characteristics include:

Independent and Instructional Levels
- ❑ Rhythmical, expressive oral reading
- ❑ Accurate observation of punctuation
- ❑ No evidence of lip movement, finger pointing, or anxiety about performance

Frustration Reading Level
- ❑ Abnormally loud or soft voice
- ❑ Word by word oral reading
- ❑ Finger pointing
- ❑ Lip movements

When doing an inventory, be sure all materials are ready and at hand. Have a tape recorder ready if you have access to one. To find the listening comprehension level, begin reading the next passage to the student, asking comprehension questions. This level is usually different from the reading level, since students are able to comprehend information presented orally at a level higher than the written form. Record this anecdotal information for later reference when planning or when communicating with your children's families. A good text to see these differences for the various subject areas in reading from first grade to college is Qualitative Assessment of Text Difficulty (Chall, Bissex, Conard, & Harris-Sharples, 1996).

Mathematics Assessment

From the beginning of the year through the end of the year, you can assess students' understanding of mathematical skills, concepts, and vocabulary, using materials right from your mathematics series. We will use the Houghton Mifflin 2000 Mathematics series as an example. Both free response and multiple choice tests are provided in this series. The results of these tests can help you assess whether students have the necessary prerequisite skills and knowledge to be successful with this year's materials. The assessment materials give you valuable information about your students' prior knowledge of math at the beginning of the year, understanding of new mathematical content, and progress at report card and parent conference times. Math Steps (2000) is designed as a tutorial resource for teachers. It contains a complete battery of tests focusing on computation such as Readiness Tests, Monthly Practice Tests, and End of Year Tests. A diagnostic chart with each test shows which math standard each test item assesses, where the standard was taught in the book, and what materials you can use for intervention and remediation. Teacher materials include a script indicating how to give the tests, answer guides, and record sheets.

The computational skills tutorial which comes with the Houghton Mifflin series is an individualized diagnostic and prescriptive program designed to help all students master operations with whole numbers, fractions, decimals, ratios, and per cents. It is a total package that includes all the materials you need for pre and post testing, instruction, practice, and record keeping. The items on each computation test cover the appropriate computational standards for each grade level. This series also has test sheets, such as "Do you remember?," which engages students in grade level materials they should already know, and "Try these," which is material you can use to assess extended thinking for those students who are above grade level. Each of these provide scores you can incorporate in individual student profiles.

You may also have access to publications such as Alternative Assessment: Evaluating Student Performance in Elementary Mathematics, published by Ann Arbor Public Schools (1993), which focus on grade level and content area. This set of tests includes scripts and scoring guides which make them easy to administer and fit generally accepted math strands. These are especially useful for lower grades and provide scores which you can use along with other information when meeting with parents and families at conference time.

3.2 Exercise for Your Journal:
Two Math Assessments

A. Your school or teacher resource center will have copies of the National Council of Teachers of Mathematics: Principles and Standards 2000. Use these standards to guide you toward realistic expectations for your students in math, regardless of the grade you are teaching. The standards span Pre - K through grade 12 with expected skills and concepts for each grade level.

Refer to your grade level and use available math texts to select sample lessons and activities to engage your students as you assess their math skills. Reflect on and write a page about how effective this method is for getting to know your students. Include what you would do differently when using these standards in the future and how you might communicate your findings to parents.

B. Another assessment tool is the diagnostic interview. This is time consuming and not recommended at the beginning of the year except with students whose ability is puzzling to you. Present some problems from previously taught material and then follow this by asking for the student's answer and an explanation of how the student arrived at that answer. Conduct several interviews with students you have selected. Write in your journal what they taught you both about their mathematical thinking and about conducting interviews for assessment.

HOW YOUR STUDENTS FEEL ABOUT LEARNING

Another aspect of learning is how a student feels about herself as a learner. The attitudes students have significantly influence their learning. Students having difficulty learning or with a history of learning problems will often see themselves as poor learners and may give up working on problems which they feel are difficult, sometimes not even trying to work on them. Sometimes the problems students have, in math for example, can be traced to negative attitudes expressed by adults and low expectations from previous teachers who exhibited gender and racial prejudices. Students who feel themselves to be good learners will often plunge into a problem as a challenge and persist until they solve it. You can interview students and get at many of their attitudes informally. You can also use formal attitude scales to learn more about individuals or the whole class. Here is a list of strategies you can use to begin to get to know these attitudes. You can use the same kinds of strategies for reading, science, math, and other subjects.

Activity 3.2 Strategies to Get to Know Your Students' Attitudes Toward Learning

You can create a simple inventory yourself in which students complete sentences such as those listed below. Ask these questions for one or two subjects at a time to get focused information. Keep the number of sentences small. Five to ten items is plenty since you will have to devote time to reviewing and reflecting on student answers.

- When I do math, I feel. . . .
- My favorite part of social studies class is . . .
- What I like least about reading is. . .
- Compared to other subjects, art is. . .
- Science class is important because. . .

Another approach to get at feelings is to have students mark responses such as always, sometimes, never, to statements like "I feel sick when I have a science test," "I think reading is easy," or "Even when I try hard, I get wrong answers."

Lewis Aiken (1972) designed a scale that asks upper grade students to respond on a continuum about what they like and dislike about math. This is an excellent example of the kind of published profile available in most periodicals for teachers, such as *Teaching Children Mathematics.*

Make up an observation checklist in which you keep track of the amount of choice time students spend on reading and math activities.

Use anecdotal notes over the first few weeks to record details you cannot fit on a checklist. Note how persistent students are when working on math problems they think are hard or how easily they are frustrated and quit. Write comments such as "Joe demonstrated two ways to add 32 and 46 with models and showed pride in the work he completed."

RECOGNIZING AND NURTURING THE STRENGTHS OF YOUR STUDENTS

Look for the strengths and talents of each child and try to build learning opportunities that use these strengths and talents to learn new skills and concepts. The contributions of Gardner (1983) can be helpful in organizing the information you gain about the students through observation and informal assessment. Gardner's Multiple Intelligence Theory has been used by teachers as a guide for focusing on the many ways students and adults can be gifted. Gardner described seven intelligences in 1983. These are linguistic, musical, logical-mathematical, spatial, kinesthetic, interpersonal, and intrapersonal. Recently added was an eighth intelligence, the naturalist. You don't need an inventory, but good observation skills can help you notice certain tendencies of youngsters in your classroom.

3.3 Exercise for Your Journal:
Observing Your Students' Strengths

Choose five students as the focus of observation over a one week period. List the noticeable behaviors that students exhibit repeatedly. These are clues to their strengths:

- the student who doodles naturally uses his spatial intelligence
- the student who hums or sings frequently – musical
- the student who talks too much – interpersonal
- the student who wiggles and jiggles – kinesthetic
- the student who daydreams – intrapersonal
- the student who loves bugs and chases other kids with them – naturalist
- the student who reads all the time – linguistic
- the student who is good with numbers - mathematical

Thomas Armstrong (2000) has developed an excellent book about activities which help you and your students pinpoint learning preferences using these intelligences.

Use your observations to help you gain more knowledge about how the students in your room learn best. While it is not wise to rely on one source alone to acquaint you with the styles of the students you are getting to know, combining the information you gain with what you learn from other sources will allow you to more accurately identify ways you can best help your students learn. Tap into your knowledge about their styles and preferences to make learning easier and more relevant to their individual needs.

Some learners, for example, may have trouble remembering the basic addition facts in second grade. Three students may need three different kinds of practice to be able to rapidly recall these facts.

- ❏ One student may need to review flash cards repeating the fours only until they are all memorized before going on to the fives.
- ❏ Another learner may do better mixing all the single digit facts while reviewing them.
- ❏ Yet another learner may need blocks or cubes to manipulate to facilitate their recall.

Use your assessment information to group the students as needed. The decision of how to divide youngsters into groups will vary from project to project depending on your goals and objectives. You will want to develop a range of large group and small group activities to add variety to the school day. Traditional classroom groupings have well-known advantages and disadvantages. Group students by ability temporarily to help them master a specific skill or concept. At times, the students may want to group themselves based on interest, especially if doing projects on topics they choose themselves. Whatever the group, change the groupings frequently during the year to avoid positively or negatively labeling students or groups.

The more detailed your planning for the different abilities and styles in your classroom, the fewer behavioral issues you will have. This is just one more reason for getting to know your students. When all the students have the same assignment, the lesson must account for the varying amount of time students need during class. Be sure to plan for those who are unusually quick or those who need lots of extra time. Provide some choices for those who finish early, but tell them what they are before they begin working on an assignment.

3.4 Exercise for Your Journal: Observe Students During Free Time

Observe how students choose to use their free time and add this information to your journal. You may want to use some of the activities listed below for their choices.

The more you can build your assessment and observations into your regular classroom activities and routines, the more efficient you will be at getting to know your students and helping them to organize their time. The top choices of activities of veteran teachers interviewed are listed here:

Books from the class library or school library can be placed in a quiet area of the room with pillow or carpet squares for students to read for short periods of time. Keep a variety of books handy on many different reading levels. Choose from fiction and non-fiction. Whenever possible, get books that are related to the lessons you will be using. Change your books often. Even those you keep in your room or from your own personal library should be put away in a closet for awhile so they seem new if they reappear.

Keep quiet card games and board games on a low shelf where students can get them whenever they want to. A regular deck of cards can be used to play "War," where students win the cards each person puts on the stack if theirs is the largest number. You can make cards related to your studies for students to play concentration. They have two sets of identical cards or corresponding cards, which they place face down on the table or floor. They turn them over two at a time. The purpose is to turn over two identical cards at the same time and keep them. The beauty of this card game is the fact that you can use basic addition and subtraction facts in first and second grade, multiplication in third grade, division in fourth grade, fractions in fifth grade, and geometry and measurement in sixth grade. You can match states and capitals, vocabulary words with their definitions, and so on.

Students can continue unfinished work from a previous assignment or work independently on a long term project. This opportunity will be a function of the kinds of projects and units you use.

Try to obtain a tape recorder that has one or two sets of headphones. Set this up at a desk or table, preferably with carrels. Here even very young students can listen to tapes with headphones by themselves.

Many classrooms have one computer for the whole class. You can get more use out of it if students can work on the computer using educational software during free time.

Encourage students to write a story, poem, or draw a picture when they have extra time. Keep materials out where students can access them themselves and begin work without consulting you.

Your observations and the child's work can contribute to your knowledge of the students in your room. Your introverted students need your help in developing their interpersonal skills. Students who tend to be quiet may actually prefer to speak up more but are often hesitant. Even if they prefer to be quiet, they need to be able to communicate in groups as students and as adults in life. If you can help them strengthen their interpersonal skills during their time in your classroom, you will be doing them a great service.

When you are getting to know your students, ask questions to which everyone will have a response. When you ask what they want to learn, let them know that there may be several people with the same answer, but you want to hear from everyone. Remind students that they all know different information. Create a climate where students don't ridicule someone who wants to learn something others may already know.

You can more easily meet the learning needs of your students if you encourage them to become experts in a specific area. Cooperative learning uses the term "expert groups" to designate different contributions to a jigsaw, a group learning project (Johnson, Johnson & Holubec, 2002). This is a way you can give every student a chance to be the expert.

Activity 3.3 Social Studies Scenario Using Cooperative Jigsaw

1. Have groups or pairs read, study, or develop a specific passage, problem, or step of a project. The pairs can help one another develop their understanding.

2. After becoming expert on their topic, this pair or group teaches what they have learned to others in small groups or the class as a whole.

3. When your class is studying about another country, students can choose research topics such as geography, customs, foods, games, or language as the focus for developing expertise. Once everyone completes and shares their research (and you fill in the gaps as needed), the jigsaw becomes a complete picture for everyone.

YOUR STUDENTS OUTSIDE OF YOUR CLASSROOM: OTHER CONTEXTS IN THE SCHOOL

We also encourage you to observe your students in a variety of different contexts in the school — hallways, playgrounds, lunchroom, and specialist classes, such as physical education, art and music. The exercise below will help focus your observations in one of the many settings outside of your classroom.

3.5 Exercise for Your Journal: Playground Observation

Observe your students during free time, before school, and at recess. Put your thoughts down on 3" x 5" cards and keep them in a file with separate cards for each student, or use pages of your journal with a page for each student.

Notice those who are successful at organizing games. Make note of those leadership skills. Watch for those who stand to the side or play alone. Do others try to include them or are they forcefully excluded? How is conflict resolved? Some children are able to peacefully work out differences, but others may resort to namecalling or punching and kicking in anger and frustration. Teachers and aides will have to intervene at times. Who is it that asks for adult assistance? How do they relate to the other adults? Are they respectful? Look for skills that can be an aid to learning in your classroom. Observe those who are versatile: who engage in many different kinds of activities and can get along with many other children.

Use the observations you've made to help you understand children's behavior and learning styles. For example, try to ascertain the underlying reason why a child is an isolate on the playground. Decide to help her to be better accepted by her classmates. Some students may need help developing more acceptable social skills. Others just need encouragement and confidence-building experiences. Create opportunities for them to be successful in your room every day. These opportunities can positively influence a student's social development. Work from each student's strengths after you've completed your assessment. Giving them leadership roles you believe they can handle in school will help to increase their status and their self-confidence.

YOUR STUDENTS WHEN THEY ARE NOT AT SCHOOL: FINDING OUT ABOUT FAMILY AND COMMUNITY

Students will enter your classroom with a host of life experiences which will affect the culture of the classroom. Their community, home, gender, birth order, race, religion, and primary language, for example, will impact on their life in the classroom. Note the students who seem to be troubled, either when they are in your room or outside. You may find that a child who has difficulties in school isn't perceived to have similar problems at home. Learning about the life circumstances of each student in your classroom is another way of getting to know your students.

Find out what your students' home life is like. Do they have older or younger siblings? What are the characteristics of the family they live with? How far do they have to go to school? Do they walk, ride bikes, or are they driven by parents? Are they dropped off at day care before school and go to after school programs as well? Factors such as these influence the kind of day a student will have with you. The student who doesn't get enough rest or breakfast will have a harder time coping in school.

Get to know the community around your school before school starts. Subscribe to the local paper. Look for notices about holiday observances, arts presentations, and sports events. Observe the bulletin boards in grocery stores and libraries that contain notices of community events. Try to attend some of these, especially those that represent cultures that are different from your own. Attend the local church or temple or mosque and visit the shops and parks. Find out what is important to families with and without students in school. Expect to have youngsters in your class who have cultural observances and family celebrations you have never heard of. Invite students and their families in your class to help you learn more about their culture. Get to know the community in which the students live and learn about the many values their families hold. These topics are discussed in Chapters Four and Five.

As you get to know your students, you will find some with difficult family situations. You will feel a need to respond to many demands in order to facilitate their learning. If students are having family problems, their learning will be affected. If a parent or guardian is seriously ill or just away on business, behavior in the classroom may be affected. You have heard that consistency is important in the classroom; however, that consistency needs to be tempered with realistic expectations and knowledge of the whole child. Check with each child individually every day and pay special attention to those whose behavior seems to be atypical on a particular day. Let a child know that you see a difference and give him the opportunity to speak with you privately. Offer your help and remind the child that you are available later if needed.

As an adult in the daily lives of students, you are able to see changes in behavior that are cries for help of a youngster in serious trouble. Whether a child is mentally or physically abused, or neglected, if you suspect there is a problem, you are required by law to report this information. Check with your cooperating teacher or building administrator about how to follow up on concerns that you have about physical, mental, or sexual abuse, and learn the procedures for mandated reporting. Your new role includes advocating for students. There may be times when you are the only responsible adult a child can depend on.

If you have children from homeless families in your class, you will have another set of concerns. These students are often transient and may have little consistency in their lives. Assuming their situation is temporary, they may be moving into or out of your classroom during the year. You have to be conscious of doing what you can for these students emotionally and educationally while they are in your classroom, which may be a very brief period of time. Understand and accept the reality that you will not be able to solve many of their problems. Providing for basic needs, such as enough food and clothing, may be one way you can support them. Keep snacks in your room for all. Appropriate clothing, coats and shoes, for example, can be acquired with the help of the school counselor or social worker.

Some parents will be your most supportive allies. Whenever possible, they will be available when you request parental help. Even if they have to work around the schedules of their jobs, they will try their best to come to meetings, volunteer, and bake brownies. These parents will help their children with their homework and will want to keep in close touch with what's happening in the classroom. They may be interested in helping you in the classroom when you're ready to have them.

In some communities, you will find an abundance of high-achieving families, who are very concerned with their children's success and demand much from you. Even if you find these families difficult to work with at times, it is critical that you find ways to develop partnerships with them. Understand that they have their children's best interests in mind.

Parents, guardians, and other family members may be curious and even skeptical about your ability to provide for the education of their young ones. Some may feel your inexperience is a detriment to the education of the youngsters in your class. Whether you are a student teacher or first year teacher, you will feel vulnerable sometimes and even incompetent under the scrutiny of some families. Trust yourself. Build on your strengths and remember your successes at these trying times.

Most importantly, find out about the parents and families of your students. Reach out to families and facilitate their involvement in their student's education. For example, use homework assignments that families can work on together or send home weekly (or maybe monthly) newsletters about the focus of study in the classroom, news about field trips, and requests for recyclables for projects. These and other strategies for building positive relationships with families are discussed in depth in Chapter Four.

SUMMARY

Learning as much as you can about the students in your classroom is essential to your success and theirs. This chapter recommends many ways you can get to know your students very well by paying attention to how students manage the instructional tasks. You can easily embed your cognitive assessment in instruction and record your focused, purposeful observations during regular class activities. As these observations become integrated into your view of your class members, you will organize your instruction to accommodate what you know about them as learners and as individuals. We have given examples of lessons that meet typical elementary classroom content objectives and that will allow you to add to your knowledge of your students during the first day, the first week, and the first month of school. This chapter focuses on the other aspects of learning also— attitudes, one's sense of oneself as a learner, and the skills and knowledge one brings to the class. In addition, we offer suggestions and guidance on observing your students outside the classroom and in the context of family and community.

Suggested Resources

Armstrong, T. (2000). *Multiple intelligences in the classroom*. Alexandria, VA: Assocation for Supervision and Curriculum Development.

Campbell, L., Campbell, B., & Dickinson, D. (1999). *Teaching and learning through multiple intelligences*. 2nd ed., Needham, MA: Allyn & Bacon.

Charles, C. M. (2002). *Building classroom discipline*, 7th ed., Needham Heights, MA: Allyn & Bacon

Halaby, M. H. (2000). *Belonging: Creating Community in the Classroom*. Cambridge, MA: Brookline Books

International Reading Association. (2000). *A practical guide to reading assessment*. Washington, D. C.: U.S. Department of Education, Health Communications, Inc.

National Council of Teachers of Mathematics, (1995). *Assessment standards for school mathematics*. Reston, VA: National Council of Teachers of Mathematics.

National Council of Teachers of Mathematics (2000). *Principles and standards*. Reston, VA: National Council of Teachers of Mathematics.

CHAPTER FOUR

WORKING TO FORM PARTNERSHIPS WITH FAMILIES

There are many reasons for developing school, family, and community partnerships. They can improve school programs and school climate, provide family services and support, increase parents' skills and leadership, connect families with others in the school and in the community, and help teachers with their work. However, the main reason to create such partnerships is to help all youngsters succeed in school and in later life. When parents, students, and others view one another as partners in education, a caring community forms around students and begins its work. (Epstein, 1995, p. 701)

With the many tasks involved in preparing your classroom for the beginning of school, you may find it difficult to find time to think about collaborating with families. Forming family partnerships may be a topic that was not fully addressed in your teacher education courses or field placements, and your inexperience in this arena may make you anxious. Since relations with parents and caregivers are not always as simple and straightforward as we would like them to be, you may feel some discomfort in figuring out how to work with your students' families. However, parents and other caregivers are important allies and forming positive relationships with them will make a significant difference in your work with students and will increase your effectiveness as a teacher. Parents are your students' first teachers and their continuing teachers, and they have a wealth of information to offer you about their children. Many recent research studies have demonstrated that certain types of parental involvement give students a message about the importance of school and contribute to student academic achievement (Epstein, 1995; Henderson, 1987). Working with families is not only part of your new job, it is a dimension of your job that directly facilitates the accomplishment of your goals with students.

Even if you are feeling overwhelmed with the opening of school, you can begin to build relationships with families that will serve you and your students throughout the year. Create a plan for yourself that outlines ways in which you will reach out to parents/caregivers. If your plan is well integrated with your curriculum planning process, developing positive relationships with parents/caregivers will be a natural way of thinking and working from the start. You can begin with activities that are part of your contracted responsibilities (Open Houses, parent conferences) and develop some of your own activities that relate specifically to your classroom curriculum. Examples include an introductory letter home, a breakfast for parents/caregivers, a newsletter that discusses your homework policy and your literacy and math programs, and a culminating activity that includes parents at the end of a social studies unit. Try to find a colleague who is interested in collaborating with you on parent involvement activities, someone who has experience working with families with whom you can brainstorm, reflect, and discuss issues as they arise. Even if you do not have time to accomplish all of the goals you have set for yourself for working with families in your first year of teaching, develop a mindset that recognizes that reaching out to families is critically important. You will soon see that the relationships you build with parents/caregivers and the communication systems you establish between home and school will support your students' growth.

If you are student teaching, find out about your school's policy regarding parent contact for student interns. Some school systems limit student teachers' communication with parents and participation in parent conferences and team meetings. Other schools encourage student teachers and interns to interact with families in many of the same ways as teachers and consider this contact an integral part of learning to teach. In either situation, participate as fully as possible and interact with parents/caregivers in all ways that are appropriate. If your participation is limited, it is helpful to conduct some structured observations of family participation in school: attend a Back-to-School Night, a Parent Teacher Organization (PTO) meeting, a school council meeting, and discuss the school's family involvement practices with your cooperating teacher. If you can, arrange to sit as a participant or observer when your cooperating teacher conducts parent conferences and debrief afterwards. When opportunities present themselves, interact informally with parents as they drop off students in the morning or stop in to deliver information or to get a question answered. These brief contacts will give you a sense of some of the parents' concerns and will help you understand how useful communication with parents can occur during these short conversations and informal interactions, as well as through scheduled events.

In planning your involvement with the parents/caregivers of your students, try to become acquainted with each student's family. What is the family structure? What are the family's educational goals for their children? What is the family's cultural identification? What language(s) are spoken at home? What issues are central to this family at this time? Are there particular sources of family stress — recent unemployment, serious illness, an impending divorce, alcohol or substance abuse? As we explored in Chapter Three, Getting to Know Your Students, as you begin your work with families you will start to build understandings about the multiple contexts of your students' lives and the various factors that may impact a student in your classroom on a particular day.

Information about family diversity and an awareness of the variety of family structures you will encounter, will help you in your outreach efforts with parents/caregivers. Learning about a variety of cultures and the ways different cultures view child rearing practices, discipline, and family roles and role relationships, can enhance your skill in working with a diverse group of families. If you are not a parent yourself, you will want information about the parenting experience: the different stages of parenting and the stresses, satisfactions, and demands that are part of the role. Knowledge of the parenting perspective will assist you in your interactions with families and may help you to prevent potential misunderstandings. Familiarity with societal issues and social policies that impact families in this country will also give you insights into the lives of your students and help you gain a better understanding of the families with whom you work. Finally, knowledge of your school's accessibility to families and some of the potential barriers to involvement will help you understand how families regard your school community. This chapter will outline some broad perspectives that assist you in reflecting on your work with families and will then help you to think through specific strategies for building productive partnerships.

DIVERSITY OF FAMILY STRUCTURE AND CULTURAL DIVERSITY

It is helpful to think about the variety of families represented by students in your classroom: dual or single parent families, foster families, blended or stepfamilies, adoptive families, gay/lesbian parent family groups and families with parents who have joint child custody. Classrooms are becoming increasingly diverse as the demographics of American society change. In 1998, according to U.S. Census Bureau projections (as cited in Berger, 2000), 26% of all youths lived in single parent families. Sixteen percent lived in blended families, and 6% in extended families. Statistics from the Census Bureau (as cited in Berger, 2000) also reveal that a significant number of children are being raised by grandparents and other relatives. Classrooms reflect greater cultural and linguistic diversity. As an example of how such diversity is represented, one elementary teacher looked at the families of students in her classroom:

- ❏ 8 single parent families
- ❏ 1 family with joint custody
- ❏ 12 two-parent families, 7 of whom are dual working families
- ❏ 3 adoptive families
- ❏ 2 blended families (stepfamilies)
- ❏ 1 gay/lesbian parent family
- ❏ 1 foster family
- ❏ 2 families in process of separation/divorce
- ❏ 4 families in which English is not the language spoken in the home
- ❏ 1 family who recently immigrated to the United States

Do you think of this wide range of families when you plan your curriculum, send notices home, articulate your expectations for homework? Is this diversity of family structures and cultures part of your mindset and reflected in your classroom environment, in your curricula, in the materials you choose, and in the vocabulary you use in talking about families? Are you modeling the perspective of diversity as the norm to your students? Do you reach out to all of your students' families and try to get them involved, or do you have preconceived ideas about how some families might respond to your overtures? Several research studies have demonstrated that when teachers take the initiative to reach out, families are more involved with their children's schooling, regardless of their social class or family structure (Epstein, 1986; Epstein & Dauber, 1991).

4.1 Exercise for Your Journal: Family Diversity

Analyze the following vignette. You may want to jot down notes in your journal or use this vignette to analyze other practices.

You are planning an art activity for your class in the middle grades to make cards for Mother's Day. You prepare an integrated lesson on the roles of women who are mothers. You include mothers who are home full-time managing their families, mothers who work away from home, and you are careful to include mothers who are single and those whose careers are in traditionally male areas. As a culmination, you have carefully prepared material so each of your students can make an attractive card. The unusual paper you've bought instead of construction paper and paint is expensive so you chose not to buy any extra. You've spent two days on the art work when one of your students asks for materials for a second card. You inform the student that there are no more materials, that each person has enough to make a card for her mother or caregiver. Frustrated, you ask what happened to the materials originally given to the student for the project. The student informs you that she has two mothers and needs to complete a second card. The next day, the lesbian couple visit your classroom with their daughter who was upset about being allowed to make only one card.

- What is your response to the family?
- In the future, what could you do differently that might prevent the above situation from occurring?

As we have noted, you will be working with a wide range of families in terms of socioeconomic status, racial, ethnic, and linguistic diversity and family structure. As a first step, it is important to understand your own cultural and educational background, communication style, and your own personal biases. This self knowledge will make you more effective in building relationships with families. It is also important to seek out information and current research about family structures and lifestyles; this information will help you in reaching out to individual families and will assist you in figuring out multiple ways that families can connect with the school. One-size-fits-all family involvement programs will not fulfill the needs of a diverse group of families.

You will want to build your knowledge base and understanding of the different cultures represented in your school community. You will build these understandings over time as you get to know the communities in which your students live, and as you interact with your students and their families. Culture-specific information can help you understand the underlying values and beliefs that define the practices and customs of a particular culture. This kind of understanding goes beyond knowledge about holiday celebrations and foods. Knowledge of the ways a culture views concepts of time, family, sex-roles, authority, and health and healing will give you insights that will help you better understand your students' families and their views of the world. For example, some Southeast Asian cultures do not share beliefs common in the United States regarding the "singling out" of individuals in society for the purposes of providing special services. Different child-rearing practices, different views of role relationships in the family, and different concepts of family pride may impact a family's reaction to the screening and diagnosis and placement of students in the special education system (Lynch & Hanson, 1998; Morrow, 1987). Understanding these cultural differences will help you in your work with families.

INFORMATION ABOUT PARENTING

If you are not a parent yourself, you will want to further your understanding about parents' perspectives, to better understand some of the stresses of parenting, and to learn about developmental stages that parents go through as their children grow and develop. Living with a five year old is quite different from living with a twelve year old, and the issues that parents deal with at each stage of development change (Galinsky, 1987). These life stages may influence the kind of involvement parents seek in their child's schooling and will influence the way students want parents to be involved. The middle school child who loved having a parent visibly present when she was in third grade may be totally embarrassed to have a parent in the school at all when she is in seventh grade. This is a very difficult adjustment for parents who are accustomed to being involved. The empathetic teacher needs to be sensitive to the feelings of the students and the parents and needs to think about ways to provide meaningful involvement without requiring physical presence.

Parents experience many stresses in raising children and may not have enough time in each day to meet the multiple demands placed on them. A request that seems simple to fulfill in itself can overwhelm an already burdened parent. Sometimes, parents who are trying to meet too many demands simultaneously will ignore or forget a teacher's request. They will not be able to assist with a homework assignment, will not be able to contribute a certain material to a classroom project, or will forget to sign the field trip notice. This does not mean that a parent does not care about their child and is not supporting their child's education; it may mean that the parent is temporarily overburdened or dealing with other family, work, or educational issues that have to be given a higher priority at the moment. Family members often feel guilty that they cannot fulfill all the expectations placed on them every day.

**4.2 Exercise for Your Journal:
    The Parent Perspective**

Interview two of your friends or relatives who are currently parenting different-aged children in school. Ask them to describe a typical day in their lives as parents.

- What are the demands of the parenting role?
- What are the satisfactions and stresses of the role?
- What stages have they gone through in parenting?
- What role do they play in their child's schooling experience?
- What level of ongoing involvement do they have with the school and with their child's teacher?
- What kinds of support does the school offer parents?

You may also want to acquaint yourself with some of the parenting literature listed in the resource section of this chapter and with some of the common issues that parents experience in raising children. One beginning teacher reported, "I was so surprised when parents asked me questions about parenting issues that were not related to reading and math, questions that had to do with sleep disturbances, nutrition, discipline, and monitoring television viewing." Parents may look to you as experts in child development and may ask you questions about parenting. Even though you are not necessarily the appropriate person to answer many of their questions, you want to have familiarity with the issues and be able to refer them to other resources and other professionals. Some teachers keep files of relevant articles on school related topics and on developmental learning issues that they have collected over the years. They share these with families when an issue comes up in a conference or conversation or include them as part of a classroom newsletter.

IS THE SCHOOL ENVIRONMENT WELCOMING TO FAMILIES?

Schools and school systems vary greatly in the ways they reach out to parents/caregivers and in the messages they convey to parents about collaboration and involvement in their child's schooling. As a beginning teacher or a student teacher, it is useful to understand how your school reaches out to parents, what are considered acceptable and unacceptable ways of involving families, what school policies mandate about home/school communication, and what informal and formal customs have developed regarding home/school relationships.

Tour your school as though you were a parent and experience the environment from a parent's point of view. Some schools give visible signs of welcoming parents. Other schools give a more institutional and impersonal impression, making it more intimidating to enter the school and navigate the corridors. Many schools are locked for security reasons and can be entered only through one main entrance. Entry is more welcoming at a school that has a clearly labeled entrance with instructions to ring the doorbell, and where there is a quick response to visitors. It is also helpful to have signs at the entrance that warmly greet parents and visitors and direct them to an office in which they can obtain information. If there are several major language groups represented in the school, signs written in multiple languages may help parents feel they are part of the school community.

For a parent, the response of the school secretary or receptionist is critical. Observe and listen to interactions between office staff and parents. Think about how these interactions might make parents feel. A warm greeting and helpful and respectful attitude sends a clear message to parents that they are welcome in the school. If the secretary takes time with parents and tries to fully respond to their inquiries, they are more likely to feel comfortable and to feel they belong to the school community. It is also helpful to have teachers' names and grade levels posted on classroom doors and signs, written in the major languages spoken in the school community, marking the library, computer lab, and other special rooms.

In your tour, look to see if there are bulletin boards with information for families and parents, including information about school events, community programs, and community resources for families. The school may post current copies of school newsletters as well as announcements about PTO sponsored events. You might find the latest minutes from the school council and invitations to join parent committees established by the school council, the PTO, or another parent group. Some schools display a parent information bulletin board in the entry hall of the school or in a conspicuous place in the hallway, and some schools keep an information table outside of the main office with newsletters, parent handbooks, and brochures about the school and school's programs. Other schools have an actual family or parent center, a place where parents can have meetings and conversations with other parents. The center, staffed by a volunteer or paid director, may also sponsor formal and informal events for parents, and may function as a family resource center for the community. An increasing number of schools now have parent liaisons whose job is to help involve families in the school community. Often the office of the parent liaison serves as an information center for parents.

In analyzing your school's initial accessibility, notice whether the school's core values, goals or mission statement are prominently displayed. Also, note whether student work appears on bulletin boards, in the corridors, in the cafeteria, and in the entry way. Does the school openly reflect the goals it is trying to accomplish and give parents and students a sense of the learning community it is trying to create? You may also be cognizant of whether the bulletin boards, visual icons, and curriculum samples reflect the cultural diversity of the school, and whether parents from all cultural groups will feel included as they enter the school environment.

Notice whether there are other parents present in the school and take note of any parent volunteers working in the office and library or computer lab. Do you see clusters of parents who talk with one another at drop-off and pick-up time, parent assistants working in classrooms, or parents gathered for a meeting or workshop in a conference room or parent center? If parents are present in the school environment, do they reflect the diversity of the student population in terms of class, race, and ethnicity? The presence of parents throughout the school, in formal and informal roles, gives a strong initial message to new parents about how welcome parents/caregivers are in the school and suggests ways in which parents may be involved.

**4.3 Exercise for Your Journal:
      Is My School a Welcoming Place for All Families?**

Tour your school at two or three different times of the day. Use your journal and answer the questions raised above as you complete your walkabouts. Analyze your environmental data. Do you think families feel comfortable in this school environment? Why or why not?

FAMILY INVOLVEMENT PRACTICES IN THE SCHOOL CULTURE

An analysis of your school culture may help you determine the prevailing attitudes toward working with parents. Your school may give a strong message that parents are included in the educational process and are welcomed in the school at any time; may give the message that parents represent an intrusion or disruption for the school, and are invited to school only to participate in prescribed kinds of activities; or may give an inconsistent message, dependent on the specific classroom teacher a child has during a particular year. It is important to understand the school's and administration's attitudes towards working with parents. This understanding will help you find allies that can support your work with parents and will help you better understand some of the reactions you may get from parents as you reach out to them. It may also help you understand the reactions you get from other teachers if you use strategies in working with parents that have not previously been a part of the school's repertoire. Remember, there has been much research in the area of home/school connections in the past five to ten years, and these current perspectives were probably not part of every teacher's education. Also, individual building administrators differ greatly in their practices and philosophies of forming partnerships with families and in the messages they convey to their teaching staff about working with families. Some encourage, support, and reward teachers' work with families and take a leadership role in initiating family and community collaborations. Other principals only pay lip service to the idea of parent participation.

4.4 Exercise for Your Journal: Teachers' Room Conversations

Observe in the Teachers' Room as you did in the exercise in Chapter Two; spend 10 minutes in the Teachers' Room at three different times during the week. This time focus on issues around parent involvement. Jot down any conversations that you hear teachers engaged in concerning family involvement. Also record any other comments you have heard during the week from teachers or staff on the topic of working with parents or family involvement.

- How do other teachers describe students' families and their interactions with parents?
- Are particular kinds of families valued more than others?
- Is parent involvement an integral part of school life or is it viewed as an add-on?
- Are there great differences in opinion as to the value of forming partnerships with parents?
- In what ways do you see evidence of collegial support in working with families?

Does this exercise raise issues of confidentiality regarding private information? How is confidential family information shared? Does the school administration address this issue with teachers and staff at anytime during the year?

4.5 Exercise for Your Journal: How Does the School Support Family Involvement?

Interview two or three teachers about family involvement structures that exist in the school. If possible, interview one of your school administrators.

- How does the school reach out to parents?
- How does the school communicate with families?
- How and when do individual teachers communicate with parents?
- When are parents and families invited into the school?
- Do parents volunteer in the school? If so, in what ways?
- How do families support student learning at home?
- Does the school offer educational programs for parents/caregivers?
- What are the expectations for teachers in terms of family involvement?
- Are teachers evaluated on their skills in working with families?
- Does the school recognize family diversity and actively reach out to all parents?
- How does the administration support teachers around family involvement?
- Does the school collaborate with other agencies to provide services to families?

From the three exercises above, analyze your school environment in terms of whether it is a welcoming place for all parents, in terms of the ways teachers talk about families and family involvement, and in terms of your observations of administrative support for family involvement. If the school culture actively supports family involvement, you may have many resources to help you in your efforts. If family involvement is minimal or haphazard, at best, it will be even more important to seek out other teachers who are committed to working with parents.

When Your School Actively Supports Family Involvement

Some school systems have official policies regarding parent involvement, and working with families is a high priority. These systems provide resources to support teachers in their work with parents and families — training for teachers in communication skills and conferencing, parent and community liaisons, translators, release time for teachers for parent conferences, space (family center or office for parent liaison), and regular family newsletters. One school system even funded a public awareness media campaign in the community urging families to become involved in their children's schools and urging businesses to give workers the flexibility to become involved and to attend their children's conferences. Such systems have built the underlying structures and activities to support family involvement. These may include:

- a back-to-school picnic
- orientation meeting for new parents to acquaint them with school policies and the curriculum, and to give them an opportunity to meet other parents and get acquainted with the staff
- parent handbook
- regular school newsletter
- school web site
- parent teacher organization
- informal social events such as ice cream socials, spaghetti dinners, informal coffees with the principal
- school performances to which parents are invited as audience
- information sessions on special education services
- school council or advisory body which includes parent representatives
- opportunities for parents to volunteer in the school: assist in the library or classroom, work in the school office, chaperone a field trip, organize a book fair or other fundraiser, share special expertise
- parent evaluation form that is analyzed each year and results are reported to the school community
- opportunities for parents to learn about the curriculum, for example, family literacy program or family math night
- room parents
- interpreters
- opportunities for families to learn how to support their children's education at home
- inservice workshops for teachers on communication skills, parent conferencing, working with diverse families, community service support systems, family involvement
- parent education programs jointly planned by parents and school staff and based on needs identified by parents
- parent/teacher/administrative task forces and committees, including hiring committees

❏ regular parent/teacher or parent/teacher/student
conferences with some release time for teachers
❏ administrative leadership that supports family involvement
❏ parent/family liaison
❏ before-school and after-school programs for students
including an after-school homework center

If your school has created some of these structures, it is easier to support the parents/caregivers of students in your classroom. These systems also offer families a variety of ways to be involved in their children's schooling, and they can pick and choose the activities that meet their needs, comfort level, and availability.

As a new teacher, if you find yourself in a school that has a high level of family involvement, you may feel somewhat intimidated. You may not be ready for all the levels of involvement that may immediately be demanded of you. The scenario below is an example of such a situation. How can you solve this dilemma without alienating your classroom parents? To whom can you turn for advice and counsel? Is there a compromise plan of action that may satisfy some of the needs that parents are expressing?

4.6 Exercise for Your Journal:
I'm Not Ready for Parents in My Classroom!

You are in your first year of teaching, and it is the beginning of the year. The first three weeks of school have had ups and downs, but for the most part you feel as though you are holding your own. You are beginning to know your students and have begun to build a climate that feels like a classroom community. It still is a bit precarious at times, but students seem to be getting along with one another and are feeling a sense of belonging to a group. You are beginning an in-depth study in social studies in another week and have been working hard on planning the unit.

You have had several requests from parents regarding working in your classroom. You believe in parent participation, and you have had many positive interactions with families in informal ways this year. But you are not ready to have parents working in your classroom. You need more time with the class yourself. You have noticed that some of the other teachers have already had parents volunteering in their rooms. It seems as though some parents expect to spend a lot of time in their children's classroom. It also seems that parents want to check out the "new teacher," and you are feeling tension from some of the parents. How should you handle this situation? Write your thoughts in your journal.

When Your School Does Not Support Parent Involvement

If your school does not have structures in place to support family involvement, it is much more difficult. Susan Moore Johnson (1990) observes, "Many (teachers) have found that they cannot forge successful home/school alliances on their own. Those who worked in schools that systematically shut out parents had found their independent efforts to solicit opinions and assistance from parents ineffective," (p. 82). In this case, it is important to find other teachers as allies. Support from other teachers can be critical to the success of the activities.

One veteran kindergarten teacher reported that she offered Saturday curriculum events four times a year to her students' families. The sessions were informative, were well attended, and helped families support student learning at home. When she changed schools within the system, she instituted the same kind of events. However, she encountered much hostility from the other teachers in the building, who were fearful that they might be forced to offer similar workshops. It took her two years to build the kind of trust and support from colleagues that enabled her to comfortably offer these curriculum sessions.

If you have assessed that you work in a building in which many of the teachers and administrators do not try to reach out to parents, you know that your own efforts may be more difficult. Do not fall into the trap of blaming parents or families for not participating in school activities, especially if you have observed that the school is not a particularly welcoming place to families or if you work in a school that basically shuts out genuine family participation. Do not think that parents who don't seem involved in school do not care about their children or their children's education. There are many reasons why parents and caregivers are not comfortable coming to school:

❑ past schooling experiences of their own that make them feel uneasy in a school setting

❑ past experiences with the schools in which only negative messages were conveyed to them about their children

❑ past experiences with the schools in which they were treated in a patronizing way

❑ work schedules that do not allow them to attend school events

❑ lack of child care

❑ families with no transportation

❑ cultural values that clearly separate the work of parents and teachers so that it would be disrespectful for parents to interfere with the work of teachers

❑ families in which English is not the first language and it is difficult to communicate with teachers and school officials

❑ families that are overwhelmed with survival issues: housing, food, health care

❑ families experiencing a crisis situation

(Finders & Lewis, 1994)

It is best not to make assumptions regarding why families may not be involved, but to work as closely as possible with each family to understand how to best make contact.

As we mentioned above, if there is little support from the administration of your school for working with families, try to find allies in other teachers or specialists, even if there are only one or two. If you are completely alone in your efforts, try to find some support outside of the school, preferably someone who is familiar with family involvement issues and who can serve as a sounding board and peer advisor. You will want to talk through situations as they occur, generate alternative solutions to problems, and evaluate your strategies as you apply them in your ongoing work with families. If your school has a parent liaison, you may have a resource who has a wealth of knowledge about family involvement in your school and who can help you with your outreach efforts with families.

In Chapter Three, we stressed the importance of getting to know your students as individuals. If you can convey to families that you know their children well and care about them and are working for their best interests, parents will be more responsive to your requests to work together. Several teachers in a beginning teachers group put major efforts into getting to know their students and students' families in the beginning of the school year. Although it was time consuming when they were burdened with so many other responsibilities, they reported that it was worth the time and energy.

> My first parent meeting was the third week of school. My parents were surprised and grateful when they realized that I knew a great deal about their child. I focused primarily on positive qualities and identified one area, or two at the most, we could focus on strengthening during the course of the year. This set a very positive tone for the year.
> (Beginning Teacher, Combined Grades One-Two)

> There was very little parent participation in my school. I kept extending invitations to parents to come in and talk with me. I would meet before or after school. Gradually parents began to recognize that my invitations were sincere, and a few parents scheduled meetings to talk about their children. As the year progressed, parents felt more comfortable, and I got to know quite a few of my student's families. These conversations helped me tremendously in my work with students and helped some of the parents support their children's learning at home.
> (Beginning Teacher, Grade Five)

Getting Into the Stream of Family Involvement

As a new teacher or student teacher you should gather information about required family involvement activities: Back-to-School Night, parent/teacher conferences, and procedures for parent review of report cards and/or portfolio assessments. Ask about other school events that teachers are required to attend or that most teachers do attend, for example, an annual spaghetti dinner, school bazaar, or ice cream social. Find out what is expected of teachers regarding participation on PTO committees. Find out if most teachers publish classroom newsletters. You will also want to learn school procedures for communicating with non-custodial parents.

You may not be able to put a large percentage of your time and energy into planning programs for parents in your beginning year of teaching. Still you should be well prepared to participate in schoolwide events. You also need to become knowledgeable about formal rules for communicating information. In some schools, the principal needs to review all communications to parents before they are distributed. As we have suggested, learn about the school culture and try to understand the unwritten norms that exist in regards to parent involvement.

BUILDING RELATIONSHIPS AND ESTABLISHING COMMUNICATION SYSTEMS

Relationships with families evolve over time and must be nourished along the way. If trusting relationships are developed, it is easier to deal with conflicts and differences in values, and to work together when a problem occurs or crisis arises (Swap, 1987). It is important for teachers to provide the lead in fostering these relationships and in reaching out to parents. As a beginning teacher, you have to work especially hard at building trust since you are an unknown quantity to parents. If you are trying to set the stage for two-way communication, it is important to model effective communication yourself. When teachers model positive, frequent communication, then parents will be more likely to respond. Making this kind of open, two-way communication the norm helps provide an information flow from home to school and back.

In the beginning of the year be available to interact with parents informally in the morning before school. Although this is a busy time for setting up classroom activities, it is also an excellent time to build informal relationships and to show parents that you welcome and value their input. Some parents may come in to drop off their children or to ask a quick question on the way to work. These informal exchanges are important to parents and to the parent/teacher relationship. As casual as they seem, they are important ways to begin building a relationship. If possible, have your daily classroom preparations completed when children arrive so that you are not preoccupied. Parents will then feel comfortable in approaching you and will not feel as though they are interrupting you. Responding in a warm, friendly and interested manner to parent questions and requests for information gives parents the initial feeling that you are interested in their concerns and in their children. An effort to get to know the family member as a person will help in establishing a positive working relationship.

Some teachers like to initiate contact with students and families before the school year begins by sending students postcards welcoming them to their class or by writing a brief letter to the family. The letter may include a welcoming message and may contain some news regarding some of the activities students can look forward to. Teachers sometimes use the letter as a way of introducing themselves and of sharing some of their own interests. Another way of reaching out before school begins is for the teacher to write to families and ask them to tell them about their children. Families can write back in whatever language is most comfortable (Weiss, 1997). Again, these initial contacts begin to give families the message that you care about them and are interested in your students.

In the beginning of the school year, parents crave information regarding their child's classroom. A new year brings new anxieties and parents often have many questions about teacher expectations, classroom organization, curriculum, scheduling of classroom specialists (art, music, physical education), homework, classroom management and discipline. The first week of school you should provide parents with some basic information regarding expectations, beginning school activities, homework, a schedule of specials, and ways that parents can communicate with you. Some teachers prefer parents to contact them through the phone and give parents call-in hours when they are available; others prefer a written note; some teachers have home/school journals they use. Electronic mail is another means of home/school communication. If using e-mail, one needs to be sensitive to issues of access and also to issues of personal preference. Many teachers and family members, even if they have access to electronic mail, may not choose e-mail as the preferred way of communicating. If you have a phone in your classroom, voice mail is another way to establish two way communication. Clear boundaries need to be set in the use of voice mail, and you may want to establish times that you are available to return phone calls. E-mail and voice mail also allow you to leave informational messages such as details about a field trip, the latest homework assignment, or a volunteer opportunity for a parent. Finding multiple ways to communicate information will keep parents informed and reduce their anxiety. Families are trying to establish their own routines at home and are looking for information from the classroom.

It is important that teachers respond quickly to parents so that their concerns are acknowledged. All too often, a parent will write a note to a teacher, and a week may elapse without a response. The parent begins to wonder if the teacher received the note because the delivery is often dependent on the student remembering to give the note to the teacher. Even if you need more time to give parents a full response or time to research an issue, a quick acknowledgment of receipt of a communication is reassuring.

A regular classroom newsletter can be an informative communication vehicle. If you are writing a regular classroom newsletter, give parents an idea about how frequently to expect the newsletters. If you have parents whose first language is not English, you may want to find a translator who can help you produce copies in other languages. Newsletters should be fairly brief, written in language that is understandable by a wide range of parents, and free of educational jargon. If you include drawings and other student work in your newsletter, be sure that in the course of a semester that you include the work of all of the children. Newsletters can keep parents informed about the classroom curriculum, of ongoing ways they can be involved at school throughout the year, and can coach families on how to support children's learning at home and in the community. Newsletters may also include articles, stories and poems written by students in the class.

One teacher, whose class all had access to e-mail at home, began writing e-mail messages several times a week, updating families on classroom studies and events. These "midnight messages" were so well received by families that they eventually replaced her classroom newsletter. Parents were delighted to receive such specific information regarding classroom activities and conversations, and the teacher found that the e-mails were a tool to help her reflect on her teaching and on daily life in her classroom. E-mails, such as the example below, were also full of ideas for engaging students in conversation at home and helped build continuity between home and school.

Hello everyone!

We are beginning some work with fractions this week. The younger children talked about fractions in reference to single sodas from a six pack (I drank 1/6, 5/6's are left) and in terms of the group (what fraction of our group is girls, what fraction of our group has shirts with stripes, etc.) The third graders made their own "fraction bars" this week (1,1/2, 1/4,1/8,1/16) and are playing some games with them which involve them in concrete comparisons and equivalencies. The fourth graders are reviewing concepts from last year and are using different materials to explore comparisons and equivalencies. Their fraction work will soon dovetail with beginning decimal and percentage work, as well. The older children have learned the terminology of numerator and denominator; all need continued talk about what each of these numbers tells us in fraction notation.

This is a good time to connect with fractions at home through various measurement activities, such as cooking, woodworking, and sewing. It is important for children to be involved in the use of fractions in many contexts, such as volume measurements (1/4 cup flour), linear measurements (3 1/2 feet long), area measurements (2 1/4 square meters) and weight measurements (65 1/4 pounds). Enjoy.

(Su Henry, Teacher of Combined Grades Three-Four)

Parents often complain that they only hear from teachers when the news is bad. By establishing regular communication channels — newsletter, frequent classroom updates, systems for families to respond so that two way communication is easy — it will be less difficult to communicate when there is an issue or a crisis. It is important to communicate good news. Some teachers try to jot a note to each family at least once a month and make a point of communicating positive achievements of their students as well as problems and issues. Some teachers have developed a "telegram" system to communicate to students' families and try to communicate several times each semester. For example, "Jamillah wrote a story with lots of detailed description about getting her new puppy, and volunteered to share her work with the class in Author's Chair. Ask her to show you this piece of writing." "John was especially kind and empathetic to Jeremy, the new boy who joined our class today, and spent time showing him around the school." A quick call home with positive information is very much appreciated and can help to build a positive relationship.

Parents also complain that they are not informed of problems when they arise and that teachers do not alert them to their children's academic and social issues in a timely fashion. You want to avoid having parents ask questions such as, "Why did you wait until the May conference to tell me that Michael is struggling with math?" or "Why didn't you contact me if Catherine was getting into fights on the playground?" As is described in the vignette below, it is often difficult for a first year teacher to know when and how to contact a parent outside of the regular conference periods.

4.7 Exercise for Your Journal: How Do I Talk to These Parents?

Linda, a first year teacher with a class of third graders, found herself especially puzzled by one child. This boy, who was new to the school this year, seemed to be constantly getting into fights with other children, particularly one other boy. Linda was concerned about his behavior and decided that it would be helpful for the parents to know what was happening. She had learned in her teacher preparation program that it was important to communicate with parents. Although she was somewhat nervous, Linda decided to call the parents. She called the child's home at night, and the father answered the phone. Linda began to describe the behavior that she had been observing. She asked the father whether the child ever engaged in this kind of aggressive behavior at home and whether he thought there might be anything happening at home that might be influencing the school behavior. The father was very curt; he denied that the child ever acted this way at home and said that everything was just fine there. He said, "Maybe you better think about what you are doing at school." Then he said that his wife might come in and talk to Linda sometime and hung up the phone. Linda was very upset. She wasn't sure what had prompted this response. Think about the situation and write responses to the following questions.

- What do you think might have caused the father to respond in this way?
- What are other ways in which Linda might have addressed the situation?
- What should Linda do now?

Establishing communication is a complex process, and you may experience tension and conflict along the way. Do not give up because you have a difficult interaction. Try to problem solve and, when necessary, obtain advice from a colleague or administrator. The school's parent liaison, the student's last year teacher or another veteran teacher, a guidance counselor or school social worker, may have advice regarding approaches to use with a particular parent or next steps to try when a strategy does not seem to work. Keep your principal informed of difficult interactions with families, and if these situations persist, seek your principal's guidance.

HOMEWORK

One of the areas that falls in the ambiguous territory between home and school is that of homework. Since homework can impact family life, it is extremely helpful to parents to provide some general guidelines and expectations for homework. Many teachers communicate their homework "policy" in the beginning of the year through a welcome packet, a newsletter, and/or at the Back-to-School Night. Parents want to know what kind of homework(or subjects); how much homework; how much time students should be devoting to homework; and what role, if any, should they play. Some parents also want to know if there is help available at school when students are having difficulty with their homework.

Some parents are looking for guidance as to how to help their students with their homework. An article in the school newsletter or a PTO event focused on supporting student learning at home provides a forum for discussing homework. Parents are often instructed to play a support role by providing a quiet place to complete homework, setting a regular time, providing supplies, and being available for advice. Some teachers request parents to sign a form, indicating they have reviewed the homework. You will want to spend time clarifying your systems regarding homework and your expectations for students and their families. You will also need to be flexible and responsive to individual family situations.

4.8 Exercise for Your Journal:
I Don't Have Time to Help with Homework

You are a teacher in a third grade class. One of the children in your class has a language learning disability. He receives help from a resource room teacher who comes into the class. You are working well with this teacher and feel that, with her help, you are able to meet his needs quite well. At this point, your major frustration is that he never seems to get his homework done, even though you intentionally give him less to do than you give the other children. You feel that his parents need to help him more at home to make sure he gets the reinforcement he needs for doing the homework. When his mother comes in for the first parent conference, you mention this problem to her and tell her that you feel it is extremely important that she or her husband help him at night. She responds that she understands that homework is important, but she has four other children at home, has a full-time job, and her husband works nights. She feels that it is impossible to help him and asks you to give him time in school to do his homework.

- How do you respond to this mother?
- Are there any alternatives that you might propose?

THE OPEN HOUSE OR BACK-TO-SCHOOL NIGHT

Many schools have established a schoolwide Open House that takes place early in the fall. At some schools this event is very well attended; at other schools only a handful of families participate. The format of these events varies from school system to school system and from elementary to middle school. The purpose of these events is to introduce families to their children's teachers and for families to gain an understanding of the curriculum, of grading policies and student assessment, of the classroom routines, of homework policies, and of ways families can be involved in the school, in the classroom, and in their children's schooling. This is an excellent opportunity for new teachers to begin building relationships with families and to present their goals for the year. This can also be an overwhelming experience, but if you are well prepared for the event, this is a good way to begin to get to know your students' families and begin to build rapport and positive relationships. In Chapter Three, "Getting to Know Your Students," we gave you many recommendations for learning about your students' interests, needs, and skills. This knowledge about individual students will help you interact confidently with parents at the Open House.

If you do not have a formal mentor that you can talk to regarding the open house, seek out an administrator or a veteran teacher for advice. Find out in advance the schedule for the evening. If families will spend a half-hour to forty-five minutes in your classroom, research the ways other teachers have organized their classroom meetings. Will you give a presentation, show a video or slide tape of a typical day, or engage families in an interactive activity or discussion? Will you have handouts or student work folders available? If you are making a formal presentation, you want to be well prepared ahead of time. You also want to think through questions that parents may ask you, and have some responses ready. If you do not feel comfortable presenting in front of groups you may choose a different strategy, but even if you are presenting for only a few minutes you will want to be well-prepared and rehearsed.

If you are giving a brief presentation, introduce yourself to parents and give them some background information about yourself and your teaching philosophy. You will want to give an overview of the curriculum for the year in each of the subject areas (or the subject) you are teaching. Parents are interested in how you assess students, your homework policies and procedures, and what a typical day or period (if you teach middle school) looks like in your classroom. Families also like information on how they can be involved in supporting their children's learning at home and in volunteer activities in the classroom and school.

Of course, you will have spent time carefully preparing your classroom environment. You want to be confident that the environment reflects your teaching practices and visibly demonstrates the kind of curricular activities that you refer to in your presentation. Even though it is early in the year, you will want to have several examples of student projects and activities on your bulletin boards. You also want to make sure that each of your students has work on display.

Parents will be checking out the "new teacher" at the Open House, and a positive first impression can go a long way in helping you build partnerships with families. Informal conversations can be as important as a formal presentation in making contact with parents. Even if you are addressing the group as a whole or planning an interactive activity, you will want to save some time for parents to circulate and interact in the classroom environment. One parent reported to another parent after attending the Open House for her fourth grader,

> I was impressed with the new teacher. She talked with us in an open manner, and made me feel as though she was genuinely interested in my son as an individual. She communicated her respect for parents as their child's most valuable teacher and invited our input and feedback. She specifically asked for our comments on homework packets and wanted us to let her know if the homework became too overwhelming. She shared with us her particular passion for writing and explained that she loved to work with students on writing across the curriculum. She also told us how to communicate with her, indicating the best way to reach her was to write a note and letting us know she would respond by the next day through a note or a phone call. I came away feeling confidence in her as an educator and feeling that she wanted to collaborate with families.

Be aware that some families may seek out information regarding their individual child's progress at this event. This kind of information is more appropriately discussed in an individual conference. Do not hesitate to set limits and to encourage parents to schedule an appointment at a different time. Some teachers create a conference schedule where parents can sign up for an individual face-to-face conference or a telephone conference. This is helpful for parents who feel an urgent need to speak to the teacher regarding their child's adjustment to school.

4.9 Exercise for Your Journal: The Open House, Reflections and Next Steps

If you are a student teacher, try to attend an Open House in your school. If you are a beginning teacher, take a few minutes after your first Open House to reflect on the evening by jotting notes in your journal. Critique this event.

- What was the parent turnout like?
- Did parents feel welcomed? Were refreshments provided?
- Was the event well organized? Did it meet the needs of families?
- Were parents notified enough in advance?
- How were they notified? In which languages?
- Was child care or transportation provided?
- From a parent or caregiver perspective, what did they get out of the evening?
- Did attending this event make families want to be more involved in their children's schooling?
- Was the evening responsive to all of the parent groups represented in the school community?
- What kinds of questions did parents ask? If these questions and concerns were not addressed at the open house, how and when can they be answered?
- What kind of follow-up will you do for the whole group? For individual parents?
- Did you accomplish your goals?
- What will you do differently next year?

As Joyce Epstein (1995) suggests, we must seek ways to redefine our home/school practices to meet the needs of a diverse group of parents. Many parents, for a variety of reasons, may not be able to attend an evening or late afternoon open house. If parents cannot attend, how can the Open House information be conveyed to them?

- ❑ send the handouts home,
- ❑ write an article about the highlights of the Open House in your class newsletter,
- ❑ send a video of the presentation home,
- ❑ have a room parent who could attend call parents who could

not and answer questions they may have,
❑ encourage families to talk with you individually regarding the Open House information.

PARENT CONFERENCES

Many parents have ranked parent conferences as an important type of parent involvement activity. Since conferences are so highly regarded by parents in terms of family/school communication, it is important to be well prepared for each conference. We suggest that you develop a clear outline for structuring your conferences. Conferences can be a daunting task for a beginning teacher because regular teaching and class preparation usually continues during the conferencing period, and the preparation for conferences requires a substantial amount of work. If you have worked hard at getting to know the students in your class individually, you will be in good position for preparing for conferences. If you have diligently observed and recorded your observations of your students as they work and interact in your classroom, you will have anecdotal information to share with parents and specific information about your students' academic progress. You will also want to take stock of your own communication style in your conference preparation and think carefully about how you will communicate with the diverse group of families that make up your class. Think about language, cultural issues, and family structure.

Elements of the conferencing experience may be out of your control. Some school systems have designated conference days and an allotted time for each individual conference. Ask in advance how conferences are set up at your school and find out how and when conference announcements and invitations are sent. Whenever possible, it is advisable to make the invitations warm and welcoming — enclose a personal note on the invitation; if a standard, bureaucratic invitation is distributed by the central administration, follow up with an invitation written by your students. Try to give choices for conference times and build in some flexibility if parents need to schedule alternative times to accommodate their schedules. Some teachers try to offer some early morning, early evening or Saturday conferences for families who can not make the designated times. In a few cases, teachers may even try to schedule conferences at a place other than the school if they know that parents are comfortable in a community setting and would not journey to school due to transportation issues, safety issues, or general discomfort in the school setting. In some schools, providing child care is one way to facilitate family attendance at conferences. Classroom aides or college students may be paid by the hour to supervise siblings in a separate space while parents participate in conferences.

You may want to make some suggestions as to how parents can prepare for conferences. Some schools send information about conference preparation in the school newsletter. In other places, teachers, in their conference invitation, include a set of questions for parents to think about or an outline of what parents can expect at the conference. Some teachers encourage parents to bring in their own questions and issues and let them know that there will be time on the agenda for this. A sample conference structure may include:

❑ Planning and Preparation:
- Invitation: place and time
- Collection of information regarding students: checklists, work samples, portfolios, assessments (formal or informal), anecdotal information, information from other school personnel who work with or who have worked with the student
- Arrangement of physical environment to make the environment comfortable for adults, and as private as possible
- Interpreter (if needed)

❑ Conference:
- Welcome: establishing rapport
- Mutual agreement on purpose of conference and agenda
- Information sharing
- Problem-solving (issue on agenda)
- Listing of next steps or follow-up with agreement on timelines
- Summary and positive closing

❑ Follow-up:
- Take notes and write comments
- Follow-up on plans as agreed
- Evaluate, and communicate back to parents

It is often difficult to accomplish everything that a parent and teacher desire in a conference period — sharing information about the child in both the home/school contexts, reviewing work for a four or five month period in various subject areas, and discussing questions or issues that a parent or teacher considers central to the student's development and progress. Often so much time is spent reviewing work folders that parents' issues are never addressed, and there is no time to engage in a thoughtful problem solving of an issue. To prevent this from happening, it is important to mutually agree on the agenda and make sure that parents' questions and issues are addressed. As Sue McAllister Swap (1987) illustrates, one teacher came up with a strategy of devoting half of the conference time to the discussion of issues that parents raise. The teacher provides parents with a tentative agenda, and then they revise it at the beginning of the conference. However the agenda gets set, teachers need to be conscious of the time and keep the conference focused.

If you have had the opportunity to become acquainted with the parent and family at an Open House, through PTO meetings, committee work, or through informal contacts at pick-up or drop-off time, you probably have begun to establish a relationship. If you are meeting for the first time for a beginning of the year conference, you will need to spend some time developing a relationship. Sharing information about yourself and getting to know the parents and the family is an important agenda item. Listen carefully to family members as they talk about their lives and the student's life at home. If you have focused on getting to know your students, much of this information will be familiar or will add to the knowledge that you already have. You also want to let the family know that you know their child well as an individual and that you are interested in their child's progress and development. Stories and anecdotes or descriptions of incidents in the classroom can go a long way in communicating your desire to understand their child and to create a feeling that you are allies, working together for the best interests of the student.

Some elementary schools have conferences very early in the year. The first conference simply gives families a chance to talk to teachers about their child and their family life and gives the teacher a chance to talk about the student's initial adjustment to school. It gives the teacher and family an opportunity to develop a personal relationship without the pressure of a full academic progress report. Even if you do not have the luxury of this extra conference time, it is well worth the time to devote a portion of your first conference to getting to know the family and let the family get to know you.

In face-to-face conferences, non-verbal messages can be as important as the verbal message that you are conveying. Be conscious of where you are sitting in relationship to the family and of your non-verbal responses. Sit at a table where you can be side by side or face to face to look at student work together. If you teach younger children, try to provide adult sized chairs. You may be used to sitting in chairs sized for first graders, but parents may be awkward and uncomfortable in child-sized furniture. Try not to use educational jargon; many parents will not understand the terminology. Avoid judgmental language and do not talk down to families. Be as warm and welcoming as you can and try to establish a feeling of partnership. Shy away from giving advice. If you are problem solving, try to generate multiple solutions with the parents and evaluate and select the best option with them. Do not take notes during the conference; you can spend a few moments at the end of the conference jotting down your notes and next steps.

Conferences can be stressful at first. The conference schedule is often unrelenting, and you may have five or six conferences scheduled in a row after a half day of teaching. Some families may seem demanding, and, as a first year teacher, you may feel that when a parent raises an issue they are criticizing you personally. It is important to try to understand the parent's perspective and to figure out the underlying message they are trying to convey. Work hard at not taking things personally and at not becoming defensive. Remember that parents are emotionally invested in their children, and it is their job to advocate for their particular child. These suggestions may assist you as you start conferencing with parents:

Develop your listening skills and other interpersonal skills. If you have not had any training in interpersonal communication, it may be helpful to review the books listed at the end of the chapter. Active listening is a skill that will serve you well, and as you develop this skill and other interpersonal communication skills, you will increase your effectiveness in conferencing. Add interpersonal communication skills to your professional development list and look for opportunities for workshops and training in this area. It is often a neglected area in teacher education programs, as well as in in-service and mentoring programs.

Role play some common conference scenarios with another teacher or a group of teachers.

Be aware of some of the common issues that parents have

raised at conferences. Be prepared to respond to statements such as the following without being defensive.

> "My child is not being challenged enough in the area of math."
> "We are overwhelmed with the amount of homework being assigned."
> "My daughter has tests in four of her subjects within a week. Don't you teachers talk to each other?"
> "There is no way I can listen to my child read for a half an hour each evening."
> "My son reports that the classroom is noisy and he can't concentrate."
> "Another child has been harassing my child on the playground."
> "Why is my child in the reading group you placed him in?"
> "No one has ever had any problems with my child's behavior before this year. We do not see any of the behaviors you are describing when he is at home."
> "Why did you give my daughter a B- on the last English paper? She has always been an A student."

Take the time to document the main points of your conferences with parents and to document important conversations. A second year teacher reminds herself,

A recent meeting with a parent reminded me of the importance of documenting what has been said in previous conversations. A parent came in to meet with another teacher and myself about his son's grade. It seemed to him that we had not been in touch with him enough about his son's efforts. When we mentioned two conversations with him specifically addressing these issues, with one resulting in his son's attendance in the after school Learning Center Program, he started to remember. Because I had not written those meeting highlights down, I decided to write two lists: 1)What will the teacher (myself) do for the student? 2)What will the parent do to help the student? I find that it is more helpful asking parents what they feel comfortable or even have the time to do, than my asking them to help the student organize or do his homework. (Beginning Teacher Journal)

Remember that building trusting relationships and getting your message across may take time. Parents are not always able or willing to hear information that teachers present because it means that they have to accept that their child can not live up to an ideal they may have for the child (Galinsky, 1987). Certain kinds of information may seem to be (even if not meant to be) a criticism of their own parenting skills, or it may elicit grief that a parent needs to handle over time. Sometimes a period of denial can be helpful as it enables a person to take in information that is difficult. Parents/caregivers may need time to deal with their emotional responses to information teachers may give them (Swap, 1987).

A teacher and parent may have two different perspectives regarding a situation, and may eventually influence each other to understand the other's perspective. This can lead to growth in both the parent and teacher and can enable them to better support the student. However, this kind of growth and acceptance may take time. Do not be frustrated if parents do not immediately see what you see. The important thing is to maintain a relationship over time and to develop ways to work together.

> I teach a combined third-fourth grade class, and I generally have my students for two years. One student in my class was several years behind his grade level in reading and writing, and he was not completing any work in class. The student often acted out in class and distracted other students. His mother was helping him at home and was doing most of the work for him. The mother refused to allow the child to suffer any consequences at school for not completing his work, such as staying in at recess time, and instead wanted me to send all unfinished class work home. I sought outside counseling advice on how to work with the parent and the child, a service that was provided by the school system After about a year and a half, I felt that I finally made some progress and built some trust with the mother. During this year, I called the parent when the child was disrupting the class and got her to come to school and observe her child's behavior. The mother began to see that her child needed additional help and was willing to let the child do his own work at school and take the consequences. I adapted lessons and created activities where he could succeed so that he wouldn't be embarrassed in front of his peers. Once the student began to do his own work in class he began to see that he could be successful and that it was alright to try and make mistakes sometimes. It took me a long time to build this relationship with the mother, but it was an important factor in being able to help the student experience success in school. (Veteran Teacher)

MULTIPLE WAYS OF INVOLVING FAMILIES

Because of the diversity of families in any given school community, it is important for the school and individual teachers to generate a variety of ways for families to be involved.

> It is not appropriate to assume that parents from dual-career families, single-parent families, teen-age parent families and blended or step-families are able or willing to participate in educational settings in the same way or to the same degree. (Coleman, 1991, p. 15)

Schools that actively reach out to families and create a variety of ways for families to be involved, will be more successful with hard-to-reach families. Joyce Epstein (1995) observes that high quality programs will look different in each school community and "that schools must tailor their practices to meet the needs and interests, time and talents, ages and grade levels of students and their families" (p.704).

Epstein (1995) has developed a framework of Six Types of Family Involvement, which are described in the next paragraphs. The bold headlines in the paragraphs below are drawn from Epstein's Chart (1995, p.704). It is helpful to think about this framework in terms of your particular school environment and the needs of your particular families as you plan your year's work with families.

Type 1 Parenting: Help all families to support children as students. Examples: Family education programs, workshops, and videos on child development issues. Family support programs for parents, such as English as a Second Language, GED, family literacy, and computer literacy.

Type 2 Communicating: Design effective communications about school programs and children's progress. Examples: Telegrams, newsletters, e-mail, voice mail, notebooks, conferences, portfolios, variety of assessments that are sent home for review and comment.

Type 3 Volunteering: Recruit parents and family members as school volunteers. Examples: Parents as school volunteers in office, library, computer lab, individual classrooms, family work weekends, gardening and playground construction projects, fundraising, committee work, organizing arts and cultural programs or special school theme days and events; volunteer activities parents can do at home such as phone calls, book order forms, making classroom materials, school newsletter.

Type 4 Learning at Home: Include families in learning activities at home and provide information and ideas for helping with homework. Examples: newsletter column with advice for reading aloud with your child, interactive homework assignments, resource list of local field trips, suggestions for extending a particular unit of study, workshop for families for supporting students' study skills at home.

Type 5 Decision Making: Include parents in school decision-making. Examples: PTA/PTO, school councils, Parent Advisory Committees, parent representatives on hiring committees, parent role in development and approval of Individualized Education Programs, parent representation on system-wide task force or curriculum committee, family advocacy groups.

Type 6 Collaborating with Community: Use resources and services from the community to strengthen school programs and to support families. Examples: volunteer grandparent program, service learning programs with local agencies, collaboration with local science museum, after-school programs with the local Boys or Girls Clubs, professional development school partnership with a university or consortium of universities.

**4.10 Exercise for Your Journal:
Family Involvement Practices**

Think about the following questions and make notes in your journal.

- What types of family involvement practices have you tried this year?
- How many families were involved and in what kinds of activities?
- How can you strengthen the kinds of involvement you are engaged in?
- Do your practices address the needs of all of your students' families?

> • How do you find support for your work in this area from colleagues inside or outside of your school?

BALANCING DIFFERENT ROLES AND DEALING WITH CONFLICTS

Sara Lawrence Lightfoot (1978) observes in her book *Worlds Apart* that regardless of the school culture in which you find yourself, there may be a built-in tension in relationships between parents and teachers. This tension is due to differences in structural roles. Parents have relationships that are emotionally intense and all-encompassing, and they view their children holistically. Teachers focus more specifically on the learning and socialization needs of children and often are trying to uphold a set of objective standards. The parent/caregiver relationship is intimate and continues over time. The teaching relationship is often limited to one or two years; teachers have to be able to disengage emotionally when the group moves on to another teacher and because of this factor bring more distance to the relationship. Parents and guardians are concerned with their individual child and advocate for their individual child's needs. Teachers have to balance the needs of the individual with the needs of the group. Both perspectives are important in working with the student, but the perspectives are different and can create some tension. Some of the more common conflicts between parents and teachers are often due in part to the structural difference in roles, If you are aware of this point, you can be more accepting of the differences, may come to appreciate the value of the two different perspectives, and may be able to more easily engage in joint problem solving.

For example, parents often approach teachers and ask them to make a special concession for their child. This request might be in terms of more challenging work in mathematics, extra material on the student's reading level, a request to move a child from one group to another, or a request for changes in the homework policy. Teachers, who are responsible for the whole group of children, may find that some of these requests feel burdensome and may perceive them to be a criticism of their teaching. However, parents and guardians are, from their perspective, fulfilling the parenting role by focusing on the needs and interests of their child and advocating for their child. Socialization issues described by teachers may not be understood or have been observed by parents or caregivers because they do not see their child in the context of a large group with a wide range of children. Parents may truly not see behaviors at home that children may demonstrate in a school environment in which they have pressure to perform academically. Therefore parents and teachers may have different perceptions of a situation. A beginning teacher describes these different perspectives in a vignette:

> My heart sank when I read the note brought in by one of my academically oriented students. It read:
>
>> "Dear Mrs. Cooke,
>> I'd like to set up an appointment with you to discuss my daughter, Jennifer. She says she's bored with school and now she gets up every morning and doesn't want to go to school at all. I'm worried about what's happening. Please call me to set up a time we can meet."
>
> As a first year teacher, this note only added to an already overwhelming sense of inadequacy at performing one of the hardest jobs I've ever undertaken. I must also mention that I am not a young teacher but a career changer who came to teaching after working many years in management in the corporate world and raising a family. I think all of this experience helped me to not panic but to take a few minutes to reflect upon what action I should take in response to this note. After thinking it over, I decided to go straight to the source, my student. We proceeded through each subject area and the topics we're currently studying and the gist of the conversation was that Jennifer was bored in math. Her reasoning was, "sometimes I get the stuff right away and have to wait for everybody else to get it too, and that's boring."
>
> Okay, now the panic, I was reluctant to jump into before, sets in. I feel most inadequate in my ability to teach mathematics, in spite of the fact that I took graduate courses and attended a few workshops in the subject prior to starting to teach. Add to this the fact that I had to reach a broad spectrum of student abilities and I honestly could not see how I was going to meet Jennifer's need to be further challenged and not alienate the rest of the class.
>
> I called Jennifer's mom and set up an appointment. We discussed the issues and came to an agreement about how to keep Jennifer challenged in not only math but other subject areas as well. After Jennifer's mother and I met, I called Jennifer in from the library to meet with both of us and agree to what we had planned. Jennifer had to take some responsibility for her own learning; some of the ways we thought she could do that was by taking some of the math challenges made available

to all the students in the classroom. If she finished her work, she was free to take on a challenge.

Another issue I saw for Jennifer was her inability to help other students when she was working in cooperative groups. Oftentimes, she would know how to do the problem almost immediately, solve it, show her answer to her teammates and then even if they didn't understand she would raise her hand and say she was done. In conversation with her mom, she agreed, she did not have patience for anyone who learned differently or more slowly than she did. I told Jennifer I felt that each member of a cooperative group in my class had equal responsibility in the group for everyone to understand the problem and its solution, before the group could be considered finished and ready to move on to something else. She balked at this at first, but agreed that she really was capable of doing this and indicated she would try.

Though I experienced some stress when Jennifer's mother initially raised this issue, through our conversation, I learned how to provide more challenge for Jennifer in math and other curricular areas. Jennifer's mother learned about Jennifer's functioning in the social context of the classroom. Together, and with Jennifer's involvement, we all grew in our understanding of how to better meet Jennifer's individual needs within the classroom setting.   (Beginning Teacher Journal)

Conflicts may also occur between teachers and parents/caregivers due to differences in educational philosophies, differences in cultural or religious values, and differences in personal histories and personal styles. Parents and teachers may have very different opinions regarding appropriate educational goals and on teaching and discipline methods. Recognizing these differences is an important first step in being able to work through a conflict. It is therefore critical to understand one's own educational philosophy and personal beliefs so as to be able to work effectively with others who have differing beliefs.

As difficult as it may be, it is important for teachers to develop skills and strategies to deal with encounters that seem negative and threatening. Beginning teachers are often easily upset by these encounters and may retreat from further contacts with some parents. New teachers may also have difficulty working with parents/caregivers who seem overinvolved. Some parents, due to their own needs — reluctance to separate from their child, unmet personal needs, insecurities, need to keep close tabs on a beginning teacher — may make demands that on the surface seem unreasonable and that are time consuming for the teacher. However, understanding the reasons for certain behaviors and attitudes, may help beginning teachers to continue to respond in a positive fashion and to continue working with a particular family (Gestwiecki, 1996).

There are several models available that may help you develop an approach for working through conflicts with families. One such framework can be found in Fisher and Ury's (1981) book, *Getting to Yes*. Confronting conflict can be beneficial. It can help parents and teachers better understand the two worlds of the child (home and school) and work in a more coordinated way to support student learning.

In some situations, it is important to set limits for parents. You can ask a parent who interrupts your class when you are teaching to schedule an appointment. You can establish weekly call-in or call-back hours. In rare cases a parent may present special challenges and you may have to ask your principal to assist you in establishing appropriate limits.

As you develop experience in working with families, you will develop strategies that are effective for your own personal style, and you will begin to see how family involvement can positively impact your students and the whole school community.

SUMMARY

Building positive relationships with families is an important part of your job. Even though your time is limited in your first year of teaching, as you may be consumed with curricular and classroom management issues, you will want to devote some of your time to working with your students' families. Just as you develop curriculum plans, design an ongoing plan for working with families. Start building relationships with parents from the beginning of the school year. Take advantage of all formal and informal occasions to get to know your students' parents. Establish clear systems of two-way communication the first week of school and let parents know that you welcome their involvement. Familiarize yourself with your school's approaches to family involvement and be aware of existing structures the school has in place to support your work with parents. Seek advice from other teachers as you approach your first evening Open House and your first round of parent conferences. Spend time planning for these events and be well prepared. As you develop skills in working with families, you will find multiple ways of involving them in their children's education.

Identify areas for your own professional development as you work with families. You may want to learn more about the specific cultures represented in your school, you may want to increase your knowledge of societal issues that families face, or you may want more information about life crises such as divorce and chronic illness, and how they may impact children. Remember, above all, that working with your families pays off and brings benefits to your students, their families, and to you, as a teacher.

Suggested Resources

Canter, L. & Canter, M. (1991). *Parents on your side: A comprehensive parent involvement program for teachers.* Santa Monica, CA: Canter & Associates, Inc.

Epstein,J.L., Coates, C., Salinas, K.C., Sanders, M.G., Simon, B.S. (1997). *School, family, and community partnerships: Your handbook for action.* Thousand Oaks, CA: Corwin Press, Inc.

Fisher, R. and Ury, W. (1981). *Getting to yes: Negotiating agreement without giving in.* Boston, MA: Houghton-Mifflin.

Galinsky, E. (1987). *The six stages of parenthood.* Reading, MA: Addison-Wesley.

Hamner,T.J. & Turner, P.H. (1995). *Parenting in contemporary society (3rd ed.).* Boston,MA: Allyn & Bacon.

Lynch,E.W. & Hanson, M.J. (1998). *Developing cross-cultural competence (2nd ed.).* Baltimore, MD: Paul H. Brookes Publishing Co.

Turnbull, A. & Turnbull, T. (2001). *Families, professionals and exceptionality (4th ed.).* Upper Saddle River, New Jersey: Merrill.

Web Sites:

Children First: National PTA
  http://www.pta.org/

National Coalition for Parent Involvement in Education (NCPIE)
  http://www.ncpie.org/

Partnership for Family Involvement in Education
  http://pfie.ed.gov/

CHAPTER FIVE

LEARNING ABOUT YOUR SCHOOL'S COMMUNITY

Learning has a chance to prosper when communities are friendly to children and to schools. Normally young people should be learning all the time, not only in school. The entire community should be a classroom, with informal experiences in the out-of-school hours contributing to productive growth. (Maeroff, 1998, p.16)

DEFINING YOUR COMMUNITY

There are many ways in which communities contribute to your students' education. As a new teacher, you will want to gather information regarding your school community and the types of learning it has to offer your students.

Your first task is to define the scope of your school community. Your school may serve families that live in the surrounding neighborhood; may serve students bussed from a variety of neighborhoods within a city; or may, as a charter school, regional school, parochial school or private school, serve students from many different towns. Your students may live in cities, suburban areas or rural towns, or in all three types of locations. Your school community may be a homogenous community or may be quite diverse in socioeconomic class, race, culture and language, and religion. Becoming acquainted with the communities from which your school draws its students will help you understand the larger socio-political environment of which the school is a part and will give you knowledge about the lives of the families with whom you will be engaged. This information will help you figure out the most effective ways of working with your students.

Knowing the make-up of your school community will also help in planning the practical details of forming partnerships with families and an effective school visit program. Even for the venerable Open House, special arrangements may be needed. If many parents live a great distance from the school and do not have access to cars or public transportation, the school may provide carpools or bus transportation for parents to attend school meetings. If families in the school community do not have access to childcare, the school may want to arrange childcare for parent meetings and conferences. If the school has a large number of working parents, PTO meetings may need to be scheduled only in the evenings. In areas where many parents work evening shifts or work several jobs, schools have found it helpful to schedule parent meetings on the weekend.

Get to know the neighborhoods or the different communities or towns in which your students live, as well as the community in which your school is housed. This is a good time to review Exercise 2.7, "Understanding the Community," found in Chapter Two. The first hand information you gained about your school's community may help you access resources to support your students and their families and to enhance your curriculum. You may find many opportunities for field trips and service learning projects that relate to classroom studies; discover community members who are interested in volunteering in the school; and become familiar with the range of community agencies, businesses, institutions of higher education, and museums that are in the surrounding community. You may uncover existing community/school partnerships upon which you can build, or you may find ways of establishing new collaborations.

COMMUNITY DIVERSITY

Communities differ in their make-up and provide their own unique contexts. Consider the following factors when becoming acquainted with your school community:

Socioeconomic Diversity

One dimension of the community with which you will need to familiarize yourself will be its economic demographics. There is much variation among communities in the type and amount of available community resources, the level of resources the parents can contribute to the school, and in the amount of resources available to families to support extracurricular activities at home. Some communities are rich in resources and opportunities for students because of the wealth of the community and because of opportunities that parents can afford to offer their children for enrichment activities, travel, academic support, and summer programs. Some cities and towns have well-maintained and well-equipped parks and recreational resources; extensive and affordable community education programs; multiple options for before and after-school programs; town athletic programs run by parent volunteers; a large selection of music, dance, art, and drama programs; and private organizations that provide tutoring and academic support activities. Other communities may have parks and recreational facilities that are in ill repair, few affordable options for before and after-school programs or for enrichment programs in the arts, and limited access to academic support activities.

> *In one town the school PTO's and the town's Educational Foundation raised a large amount of money each year and enabled the schools to hire technology assistants, repair and rebuild playground equipment, provide mini-grants to classroom teachers to support curricular projects, fund performing arts groups in the elementary schools and provide money to run the after-school athletic program at the junior and senior high schools. These "extra fundraising activities" provided items that the school budget could not afford and enhanced the educational experience of the students. Another school system's PTO struggled for three years to raise funds to build a playground for its largest elementary school.*

Because of economic differences, raising money for playground equipment, performing arts groups, and field trips may be easy for one school community but difficult for another. Many school communities have a mix of families with diverse socioeconomic backgrounds. Schools that ask parents to send in money for field trips need to be sensitive to these differences and provide alternatives for funding these trips. The school PTO or the principal may have special funds to contribute to the cost of field trips for families that don't have the resources.

Teachers also need to be aware of some of the demographic trends regarding children's economic status in this country. During the 1980's in the United States there was an increase in child poverty, and children became the poorest group of Americans. By 1986, one in five children lived in poverty (Gersten, 1992, chap. 8) and these statistics remain much the same today (Children's Defense Fund, 2000). As a teacher, it is important to understand the stresses that poverty may impose on the lives of families. These may include substandard housing or homelessness, hunger, inaccessibility of affordable childcare, and lack of adequate medical care. All of these issues may have an impact on your students' "readiness for learning." Forming individual relationships with families and understanding their strengths and the environmental challenges they may face, is one way that teachers can support all students. Schools can support families by providing a range of resources and by collaborating with other agencies to provide services. For example, schools can sponsor before-school and after-school programs for working parents, can run homework and tutoring centers for parents who are unable to help students with homework, and can send books and other materials home for families that don't have access to these resources.

Some schools offer a full range of services including a health center, child care center, counseling services, and a job-training program housed together in a single school building. "The creation of one-stop centers where the educational, physical, psychological, and social requirements of students and their families are addressed in a rational, holistic fashion is attractive to both school people and social service providers" (Dryfoos, 1996, p.18). This model of a "full service school" can make services more accessible, can provide comprehensive services to families and children in a coordinated fashion, and can help teachers focus on quality education while other agencies provide the needed support services. These models are being tried in some of the neediest communities and schools around the country.

Safety

Another issue that influences community life for your students will be the level of safety in the community, and how freely students can move around. In neighborhoods that experience a great deal of community violence, children may be more homebound, and they may be unable to take advantage of community resources. Community violence may also limit families in establishing social networks, as it is riskier to initiate social contact. Safety issues may prevent the offering of evening meetings and activities for parents and teachers.

Cultural and Linguistic Diversity

As we have discussed in previous chapters, you will want to know which cultural and linguistic groups make up significant proportions of your school's population. If many parents do not speak English as their first language, the school will need access to interpreters and written notices will have to be translated into the major language groups represented in the school. You will want to acquire information regarding the different cultural groups represented in your classroom. Recognizing that there is great variation among individuals in any culture, some of the culture-specific information can increase your understanding of the ways families relate to schools and can help you form partnerships with families. Many school communities have been greatly enriched by their cultural diversity, and some have integrated cultural celebrations from a variety of groups into the school's curriculum. Other schools have developed two-way bilingual programs, providing a second language experience for all students. For example, in one school, the students whose native language is Portuguese learn English as a second language, and the students whose native language is English learn Portuguese as a second language.

As you familiarize yourself with community resources, you may discover agencies that provide services to specific cultural groups. These agencies can often provide you with a wealth of information regarding a particular cultural group and may have access to translators and volunteers who can contribute to your classroom curriculum. For example, in one metropolitan area there were several agencies that provided services to the Brazilian community, including a cultural center which focused on the performing arts; an immigrant center which provided job training and on-the-job support; a legal services organization; a parent information center which answered parents' questions regarding educational programs; and a family network which ran preschool programs for infants and toddlers.

CONNECTING FAMILIES WITH RESOURCES

As you are planning your curricula and interacting with families, you will want to be familiar with the social networks and resources of the community in which your school is located. You will also want to investigate school-community collaborations to find out about partnerships that were established with businesses, colleges and universities, cultural institutions, and social service agencies. Does your school have a professional development partnership with the local university? Has your school contracted for services with the counseling center down the street? Does the school social worker have connections with the church around the corner that runs clothing drives every month? Can the citywide Parent Information Center help you find an interpreter for a parent conference? Does the high tech business partner that provides mentors for your students also offer technology support to the school or donate computer equipment? You can answer these and many more questions as you explore the connections your school already has with the community. You also may find new and different ways to make use of these partnerships.

Find out if your school, town, or city has a resource file of institutions, museums, historical monuments, educational facilities, health services, community agencies, and churches that are part of the community. Does this list include the natural resources surrounding your school: parks, conservation land, reservoirs, rivers, ponds, and marshland? If such a list does not exist, work with a group of teachers, parents, and community people to compile one.

6.1 Exercise for Your Journal: A Community Resource File

Using the categories below and the information from the community exercise in Chapter Two, begin to survey your community and compile a resource file. Indicate which resources have contact with the school and who the contact person is.

- ❏ Outdoor resources: Parks, hiking trails, arboretum, fields, ponds, reservoirs, conservation land, town recreation area, beaches, salt marsh, farms, dairy farms, farm stands, golf course
- ❏ Museums and cultural institutions: Museums, artist studios, zoo. aquarium, libraries, theaters, musical performing groups (symphony, orchestras, bands, vocal groups)
- ❏ Transportation: Airports, train stations, boat docks, bus depots, navy or shipping yard
- ❏ Historical sites: Monuments, historical village, historical house
- ❏ Recreational facilities: Playgrounds, soccer, softball or football fields, basketball courts, tennis courts,

> public swimming facilities, ice rinks, open gyms
> ❑ Commercial establishments: Factories, stores, restaurants
> ❑ Social service agencies: Transitional assistance, housing authority, multi-service centers, soup kitchens, homeless shelters, elder services, counseling service, mentoring programs
> ❑ Educational facilities: Schools, child care centers, after-school programs, tutoring centers, dance schools, martial arts programs, community education centers, music schools, art centers
> ❑ Religious institutions: Churches, temples, mosques
> ❑ Clubs: After-school clubs, Girl and Boy Scout troops, Girls and Boys Clubs, 4-H Clubs
> ❑ Health services: Hospitals, clinics, community health centers, HMO's, health practices, mental health centers, alternative health practices
> ❑ Government: Fire and police department, town or city halls, state capitol building, court house
>
> (Adapted from Barbour & Barbour,1997, Table 8.1)

Another good source for locating community linkages is the weekly community newspaper, which routinely lists educational, recreational, and cultural events. Some communities also publish a list of social service agencies and educational opportunities on a yearly basis. Other communities have free newsletters that contain information on what is occurring in the community each week. For example, in reading the community newsletter a beginning teacher reported seeing:

> ❑ a listing for a child development workshop for parents of adolescents
> ❑ announcements of meetings of a support group for widowed, divorced, and separated men and women
> ❑ a listing of a substance abuse hotline
> ❑ a free family concert
> ❑ a storytelling festival
> ❑ a forum about water resources in the community
> ❑ an announcement of a domestic violence volunteer training sponsored by a local agency

❏ an announcement of funding availability from the local arts council for community arts projects.

One teacher we know has developed a column in her monthly newsletter to families that is devoted to describing upcoming community events that related to current classroom curriculum units — she gave families information about special exhibits in museums, living history presentations sponsored by the local library, family concerts, and storytelling events.

Families vary in their abilities to access community resources, and agencies vary in how they reach out to families. Children's ability to benefit from community is often influenced by the social networks their families establish (Barbour & Barbour, 1997). In today's society, with higher mobility rates and with more parents of young and school aged children working, community ties may be more difficult to establish. Teachers can support parents in accessing resources. Some schools have formed partnerships with particular colleges, social service agencies, and health centers. Teachers are in a good position to work with these agencies to connect parents with community services and resources, when appropriate, and to bring community resources to the classroom.

> *A valuable resource in one city was the Community Computing Center, which provided access to technology for any member of the city. The Center was housed in the Adult Education Center in the local high school. Since many families in the town did not have access to technology, special nights were set aside for students to use computers to do their homework. Technology classes were held for both parents and students. The Center was run by an independent agency which partnered with the school system and with the town's housing authority. The agency also lobbied to create computer centers in the city's federally subsidized housing developments.*

Even if the school offers programs and services, do not assume that all families will see these programs as a resource for their children. As a teacher, you can play an important advocacy role because you see how an issue is directly affecting a student in the social context of the classroom. You are also aware of the range of services and programs that exist. You can help parents understand how a particular service might benefit their child. For example:

> *A teacher observed that a student in her class was having difficulty making friends and seemed unhappy during the school day. The student went home*

every day with her elder brother, who took care of her while their parents ran the family restaurant. The mother dropped in unannounced one day at school, and the teacher arranged coverage for her class to talk with the parent. The mother discussed the student's unhappiness and told the teacher that the student and her brother were not always getting along well in the long stretch of time before one of the parents came home from the restaurant. The teacher told her about the after-school program and persuaded the parent to enroll the daughter for a few days a week. This eased the burden of the long hours together for both older son and younger daughter and gave the daughter a context out of school in which she could begin to work on building friendships. The teacher was able to support this social skill development in the classroom.   *(Veteran Teacher, Fourth Grade)*

COMMUNITY SERVICE LEARNING AND COMMUNITY VOLUNTEERS

Even if your school is not a neighborhood school, the school itself may be a part of a distinct community and may take an active role in community life. Some teachers are involved in service learning programs and facilitate students' participation in educational activities and projects in their communities. For example, students in one school participate in activities in the surrounding community, including musical performances in the home for elders across the street from the school, yearly clean-ups in the neighborhood playground, and involvement in a community gardening project. Understanding community connections and resources can enrich curricular opportunities for your students and can provide contexts for experiential learning.

Community volunteers may want to participate in your classroom and school activities as well. Some schools have intergenerational programs in which elder citizens volunteer in classrooms; they may read with students in the classroom or serve as mentors to an individual student in the school, having regular weekly contact with the student. Colleges often provide volunteers to teach specific content areas, to serve as tutors to individual students or to run extracurricular activities or after-school clubs. Businesses encourage employees to become involved in the neighboring schools, donate resources in cash or supplies to schools in their communities, or partner with schools around particular areas of expertise such as technology. Businesses may also provide internships for students or opportunities for students to shadow employees for a day as part of a career program. Representatives from local government agencies often welcome educational outreach opportunities and will share their area of expertise with a group of students.

> *One classroom that was engaged in a study of land and water invited a volunteer from the town's Water District. She showed the class a full map of the town, its pipes and well fields and then shared a ground water model that demonstrated how water moves through the soils and how contaminants can spread to wells. The students were very interested in the model because it made the topic immediately visible.*

SUMMARY

Even though your time is limited during your beginning years of teaching, try to get to know your school community. Tour the community; find out from other teachers, school specialists, administrators, and parents about the partnerships that already exist. Seek out community resources and keep a file for future use. Whenever possible, use community resources in your curricular planning. Bring these resources into your classroom and bring your students into the community through field trips and service learning projects.

Suggested Resources

Barbour, C. & Barbour, N. (2001). *Families, schools and communities (2nd ed.).* Upper Saddle River, New Jersey: Prentice Hall.

Dryfoos, J.G. (1994). *Full-service schools.* San Francisco, CA: Jossey-Bass Publishers.

Engaging parents and the community in schools (1998). *Educational Leadership, 55* (8).

Harvard Family Research Project (1995). *Raising our future: Families, schools and communities joining together.* Cambridge, MA: Harvard Family Research Project.

Kagan, S.L. & Weissbourd, B. (1994). *Putting families first: America's family support movement and the challenge of change.* San Francisco, CA: Jossey-Bass Publishers.

Maeroff, G. (1998). *Altered destinies: Making life better for schoolchildren in need.* New York: St. Martin's Press.

Thompson, B.A. (Ed.). (1993). *Together we can: A guide for crafting a profamily system of education and human services.* Washington, D.C.: U.S. Department of Education & U.S. Department of Health.

Wade, R.C. (1997). *Community service learning: A guide to including service in the public school curriculum.* Albany, N.Y.: State University of New York Press.

CHAPTER SIX

WORKING WITH COLLEAGUES

What new teachers want in their induction is experienced colleagues who will take their daily dilemmas seriously, watch them teach and provide feedback, help them develop instructional strategies, model skilled teaching, and share insights about students' work and lives. What new teachers need is sustained, school-based professional development — guided by expert colleagues, responsive to their teaching, and continual throughout their early years in the classroom.
(Johnson & Kardos, 2002, p.13)

BENEFITS OF COLLEGIALITY

Forming positive relationships with colleagues can enhance your work with your students, be a key factor in your continuing professional development, and add tremendously to the satisfaction of teaching. Sharing ideas, pooling resources, jointly planning curriculum units and designing assessment tools, co-teaching with a specialist, meeting in a study group, problem solving with a mentor, or observing in another teacher's classroom are some of the many ways in which you may interact with colleagues in your school building. In addition to the benefits of collegiality for your personal and professional growth, collegiality can also benefit your school. As Deborah Meier suggests, working collaboratively with colleagues, not only enhances your classroom practice but also provides a model for your students, of an adult community engaged in working together (Fried, 1995). When students see adults working and learning together in a community, they perceive the importance of learning and working cooperatively. In this chapter, we will discuss ways in which your interaction with other adults in the school will benefit your students and your school and will contribute to your personal growth and development as a teacher.

Forming collegial relationships is not only helpful, but is essential for survival as a beginning teacher. Many of the teachers who leave the profession did not find colleagues to work with and to learn from during the critical first years of teaching. As Susan Moore Johnson (1990) recounts in her book describing teachers' workplaces, working with colleagues meets many of the needs of a teacher.

> *The teachers looked to colleagues to meet their personal needs for social interaction, reassurance and psychological support; their instructional needs for pedagogical advice and subject matter expertise; and their organizational needs for coordinating students' learning, socializing new staff, setting and upholding standards, and initiating and sustaining change.* (p. 156)

As a beginning teacher, you should seek support as you encounter the many highs and lows of the initial years of teaching. You will face new situations, and you will have many questions about your students, your teaching practices, and your school system's expectations for teachers. You will look to your colleagues, people who can understand the complexities of the issues you are experiencing and who have first hand knowledge of your concerns. Being able to "blow off" steam and vent with a colleague can momentarily ease your burden and help you to refocus. Your experienced colleagues can help you view your beginning teaching experiences in perspective and encourage you to learn from the errors you make. Veteran teachers were at one time beginning teachers, and they have an understanding of the developmental needs of a teacher new to the profession. You will hear teachers whom you respect as accomplished professionals reassure you that, when they were beginning teachers, they encountered many of the same dilemmas, made many of the same mistakes, and felt just as overwhelmed as you are feeling. It gives you hope that you can grow and evolve as a teacher.

Working and connecting with colleagues may be the central source of your professional development as a teacher. As we discuss in other chapters, schools do not always effectively support the professional development of teachers. Some school systems have strong professional development programs; in others, professional development ranges from being underfunded and inconsistent to virtually non-existent. There is often little time in the regular school year dedicated to teacher professional development, and what time there is, is often reserved to support system-wide initiatives. The individual developmental needs of beginning teachers are not necessarily addressed. For example, you may feel that you have a strong need for support in science, but the system-wide professional development agenda for the year is targeted for social studies. You may be a beginning teacher in a third grade classroom, struggling with concerns of how to help students with reading comprehension, but your grade level meetings are focused on the implementation of the new math curriculum.

Your colleagues can be tremendously helpful when you are seeking pedagogical advice. If you have a mentor, formal or informal, she can offer expertise and support regarding your specific, identified needs. A teacher at your grade level might offer assistance and share materials, lesson plans, and suggestions for classroom activities. The reading specialist or staff developer for language arts might be a strong support and provide resources and a sounding board for reflecting on specific lessons or discussing your concerns about particular students.

> *For beginning teachers, the advice and assistance tendered by highly skilled colleagues means that years of practical knowledge can be mastered in far less time, without the trauma and frustration of trial-and-error learning, and therefore, with earlier and greater professional rewards.* (Rosenholtz & Kyle, 1984, p.14)

Teachers also work together to coordinate student learning from grade to grade, to reinforce core values developed by a school community, to uphold standards, and institute meaningful curricular change and innovation. This kind of collegial work is critical in developing a cohesive school community and in shaping the learning climate and environment for students. These schoolwide efforts require conversation, discussion, analysis, and broad engagement and cannot be achieved by teachers working in isolation.

Once you recognize the potential benefits of collegial relationships, you need to consider how to develop productive relationships. You will encounter many different types of colleagues in your teaching experience. With some you feel an affinity of spirit and share values and philosophies of teaching. However, there will be other colleagues with whom you will find it difficult to form working relationships; you may have differing philosophies of education and may disagree with the ways in which they interact with students and parents. Learning to cooperate with a wide range of other professionals is a critical skill to develop in the school environment.

Just as there were classmates whose company you preferred and whose friendship you valued over others, you will find some colleagues in your new school more congenial to you than others.

However, whether you initially appreciate what they have to offer or not, part of your job that first year is to detect what each of your new colleagues can offer to help you grow, both professionally and personally. You may develop lasting and valuable friendships among your colleagues, although this outcome is not a necessity. What is essential, however, is that you form working professional relationships with your colleagues.

THE RULES OF THE SCHOOL CULTURE: SEEKING HELP AND ASSISTANCE

Teaching is a profession in which one engages in an intense web of interpersonal relationships on a daily basis. Yet ironically, teaching has often been called a lonely profession (Knoblock & Goldstein, 1971; Rosenholtz & Kyle, 1984) and much has been written regarding teacher isolation. Teaching norms emphasize the autonomy and privacy of teachers, and many teachers report that they have never actually observed their colleagues teaching. In most schools, there is little time built into the school day for teachers to visit one another's classrooms, for case conferences regarding specific students, or for joint problem solving or planning. Conversations in the teacher's room are often limited to social topics rather than problem solving or professional discussion, and conversations about teaching are often conducted on the fly, a brief encounter in the halls or the cafeteria or snippets of conversation while you are cleaning or setting up classroom activities.

The school culture may influence the extent to which you feel free to ask for help and the extent to which you have meaningful interactions with a wide range of colleagues. Also, the norms of teaching, the unspoken rules of the profession that you have unconsciously learned in your teacher training program, may initially discourage you from seeking the help you need. Rosenholtz and Kyle (1984) have observed, "Most teacher education programs unknowingly teach the professional ethic that it is wrong to intrude on a colleague's turf" (p.12). Beginning teachers are often thrown back on their own devices, are uncertain to whom to turn when they begin to confront common problems, and may get the message that their professional reputation is at stake if they ask for help. Beginning teachers, furthermore, may have the perception that if they reach out for help from their colleagues, they will make themselves more vulnerable and could leave themselves open to criticism (Rosenholtz & Kyle, 1984). Depending on your

school environment, this perception may or may not reflect reality.
One new teacher recounts,

> One of the things I discovered, however, was that my first few months
> in my new school would leave me feeling very incompetent and alone. I
> wasn't surprised by the challenge — the difficulty in classroom man-
> agement, the exhaustion, or the moments of doubt in teaching a new
> concept. What surprised me most was how difficult it would be to feel
> like an outsider in my new job. I was insecure and unsure of myself. I
> was paranoid all the time that my colleagues would think I was a failure.
> Most often, in the beginning, it seemed that I worried more about my
> relationships with adults than I did about the bonds I was forming with
> my students.

The norms of teacher equality and non-interference are strong within
some school cultures (Feiman-Nemser & Floden, 1986, chap. 18).
Veteran teachers may not want to appear intrusive and may wait to be
approached by beginning teachers for help. They may be willing to
give assistance but will wait for the new teacher to make the overture.
When veteran teachers were asked how they viewed giving help to
beginning teachers, they mentioned the importance of new teachers
asking for help "Don't be afraid to ask—it's flattering!" "Don't feel
like you have to know everything." "Admitting you need help shows
you are mature." Understanding the fact that many veteran teachers
have been socialized to respect the autonomy of their peers, may make
it easier for you to take the initiative and ask for the assistance that you
need.

In some schools, teaching may indeed seem like it is performed in
isolation, behind closed doors. You may initially feel like an outsider
with some of the veteran teachers. You will need to observe carefully to
find colleagues who might be allies and to find situations in which you
can engage in conversations about teaching and learning. It may seem
as though no one ever talks about the important issues, and you may
feel as though you have little in common with the majority of your colleagues. Try to take advantage of all situations that may have potential
for making contact with colleagues with whom you can learn. The
journal exercise below may help you probe more deeply to find where
and how teacher collaboration occurs in your school.

6.1 Exercise for Your Journal:
Locating Colleagues Who Will Support You

During a two week period, record observations in your journal about the kinds of conversations that occur in different types of school meetings and in gatherings of adults in the building—school staff meetings, grade level meetings, student support team meetings, Teachers' Room, study groups, and lunch conversations. (You might also want to refer back to Chapter Two, Journal Exercise 2.6, "Life in the Teachers' Room"). In what places do you find conversations about teaching and learning? Which teachers participate in these conversations? Observe and record the ways in which teachers and support staff work together. It may not be apparent at first glance that much collaboration is occurring, but when you take a closer look you will notice that many teachers work collaboratively, not necessarily with the whole community, but with a couple of other teachers. You may find that conversations about teaching do not occur in any of the places or forums that you might expect. For example:

In one elementary school, staff meetings seemed to be devoted to administrative and logistical issues. Lunchtime conversation centered around sports, movies, and social topics. Grade level meetings were often focused on the coordination of teaching resources and ordering materials. However, on closer observation, many of the teachers in the school partnered and worked as teams. In the fifth grade, two teachers teamed: one of them taught the math and science for their two fifth grade classes and the other taught the language arts and social studies. Another team of teachers, each of whom had a self-contained third grade, planned their whole curriculum together. A seventh grade teacher worked closely with a special education teacher; they carefully coordinated programs for individual students in the seventh grade math classes and often co-taught a math class together. A student support team, consisting of a guidance counselor, social worker, special education teacher, parent liaison, school nurse, and two classroom teachers, met weekly. Teachers signed up to attend these meetings and present case studies of students. The team gave the teacher suggestions for working with the student and the student's family and coordinated follow-up. The school librarian worked closely with teachers on planning curricular units, providing media resources, and co-teaching and facilitating group work in the school library.

Once you understand where some of the substantive conversations about teaching occur in your school, you may be able to find ways in which you can participate. You might present a student at the student support meeting, begin to work with the librarian on planning an integrated unit, or see if one of your grade level colleagues would like to meet regularly to reflect on and plan the next unit in the new math curriculum that your system is implementing.

Some school cultures are more collaborative in nature, encouraging professional discussion and joint problem solving. Collaboration is the norm. It is easier to find ways of asking for help in such a culture because it is the way adults are socialized to interact in the setting, and opportunities for collaboration are built into the school day. For example, a school schedules special subjects in such a way that teachers at a particular grade level have a regular meeting time each week. A weekly staff meeting occurs during the school day every Friday while students are at an all-school meeting. Practices such as peer coaching (described later in this chapter) or a "rounds model," (described in greater detail in Chapter Seven) provide regular ways for teachers to observe one another and talk about each other's teaching. These activities may seem overwhelming and even a little threatening at first and will pull you from your focus on your individual classroom. They will require extra time and energy. In the long run, these activities can provide valuable support. As a new teacher in a school environment that is highly interactive, you will need to create a balance that feels comfortable. You will want to maintain a focus on your classroom while beginning to participate in the collegial activities. As you gain more experience and begin to know and trust your colleagues, you will feel less vulnerable and will be able to participate more fully in collegial activities.

It is imperative to figure out strategies for getting help from colleagues if your school does not support or encourage this collaboration. In some cases, assistance will be found more easily outside of your school or from the Internet (see Chapter Nine), but finding professional support and developing collegial relationships is critical to survival for new teachers and to continued growth for all teachers. Be patient. It will take time to build your support groups within and outside your school district. These supports, as described below by a veteran teacher, are invaluable to new and experienced teachers alike.

We often react to the stressful and hectic days of teaching by putting ourselves on an AUTO TEACH modality. We plan, we teach, we grade, we go home. This does not happen because we are irresponsible and/or immoral professionals. It happens because we are called upon to do so much in the condensed reality of a school day. We lose sight of the larger goals sometimes, because the immediate reality taxes us with its demands. We sometimes lose sight of who we are and of those goals which prompted us to become teachers in the first place.

I protect myself from this pedagogical malaise with a group of teachers. Not just any teachers, but colleagues who know me, who know my goals, respect my point of view (even if disagreeing with it), and who are also involved in holding on to who they are while they practice what they are. This group of colleagues cares about my growth as a person and their own growth as professionals. They make it possible for me to return to school even after an exceptionally frustrating week. I know that I am known, and each one in the group knows that he or she is known and understood. I think they know me too well, but I don't feel vulnerable. I feel acknowledged, recognized in the Freirean sense.

One day during one of our professional development meetings, a consultant was speaking to us about curriculum. I did not agree with what he was saying, but I sat politely listening. Something drove me to turn around and look behind me. Everyone in my close group was looking at me and smiling. They knew that I disagreed with the presenter and were simply waiting for me to say something to him. I didn't. I didn't need to. The significance here is that a group of teachers can come together, discuss important issues, come to know one another and be the source of unending and nourishing recognition and support.

(Abraham A. Abadi, Veteran Teacher)

BUILDING RELATIONSHIPS

How do you determine if it is safe to reach out to a particular colleague? What if you ask for help, and then find that the teaching philosophy of the veteran teacher is incompatible with your teaching philosophy? How do you handle unsolicited advice from veteran teachers at your grade level that goes against your approach to teaching? Beginning teachers report a range of situations and responses from their colleagues. You may be lucky and you may have an experienced teacher take you under her wing and provide just the kind of mentoring and assistance you need. One beginning teacher remarks,

I felt extremely fortunate. One colleague who has been teaching for twenty-four years has become my mentor. We are extremely compatible, and we both seem to enjoy our relationship. She has been an invaluable resource, guide, and coach. I don't know how I would have survived this year without her.

You may, on the other hand, feel very much like an outsider and as though you will never fit in. Teachers are pleasant and may offer advice but the advice is not compatible with your goals and philosophy of education. Another first year teacher reflects,

> The veteran teachers in the primary grades have been cordial and for the most part have not given me much feedback or made many suggestions. I believe that my first graders need to engage in active learning, and I try to provide hands-on learning experiences. I have to admit that I have had management issues and a few of the students, in particular, are often not engaged and disrupt the class. I haven't developed consistent strategies for working effectively with them. A few of the veteran teachers have approached me and have told me that they too tried many of the activities that I am trying as a new teacher, and that what works well with these students is structure and direct teaching. I welcome advice about how to provide structure within an active learning environment. However, I don't see many role models for this teaching approach in this school.

In rare cases you might even find yourself amidst a group of experienced teachers who may remain cold and distant and may be resentful of a new teacher. A teacher in an university-sponsored new teacher support group describes her experience with colleagues,

> I was told when I took this job that my grade level teachers may not be welcoming. The principal warned me that this group does not like change and that two other new teachers had quit last year. Knowing this, I received ongoing support from my principal and from teachers from another grade level team. These teachers were wonderful and gave me the assistance that I could not get from my grade level team. I would not have survived the year if I hadn't found a high level of collegial support.

At the same time that you are observing the interactions of the different groups of adults in your school, you will also be involved in getting acquainted with your colleagues. The section, "Background of Your Colleagues" in Chapter Two, described ways to get to know your colleagues on a personal level. You also want to get to know your colleagues as professionals: their teaching styles, educational philosophies, areas of teaching expertise, and special talents. If you are an elementary school teacher, go to the specials with your students; get to know the art, music, physical education teachers, the librarian, and the technology teacher. Although time is limited, it is a good use of your time to approach some of the different specialists that work with your students. Ask if you can observe a speech and language session or talk to the specialist about their goals for an individual student. Talk with the parent liaison, school nurse, director of the after-school program, cafeteria workers, and custodians. Learn as much as you can about the roles of all of the members of your school community. Introduce yourself to the district curriculum specialists when they visit your school, find out the ways in which they prefer to work with teachers, and acquaint yourself with the resources and curriculum support that they can offer you. Many specialists are willing to consult regarding particular students, help you incorporate some of the strategies they use with individuals into your classroom lessons, or co-teach with you. They may be waiting for cues from you because they do not want to be intrusive.

Greet your colleagues in the morning and introduce yourself to those you don't know. Spend some time with colleagues in your building before or after school and take the initiative in asking questions and generating discussions from which you can learn. You will have some license as a new teacher to approach people that you don't know. There will be a period of time in which people will expect that you don't know the ropes, and many people will be willing to share information and assist you. Take advantage of this in the beginning of the year as a way to get to know your colleagues. If you see the same people regularly around the copy machine in the morning or on your shift of bus duty in the afternoon, begin to cultivate relationships with them. If you have a relationship built, it will be easier to approach a colleague later in the year to ask for help or to suggest that you collaborate on a curriculum unit or a reading buddy project.

Take your time in getting to know your colleagues and be patient; relationships take a while to build, and the information you gather from your observations may give you some distance that will help you with your collegial interactions in the future. It is important to realize that you are consciously building new relationships. Many of the teachers in your school may have worked together for years and have established long term friendships and professional relationships. Some schools may have social cliques. Entering a new group and establishing your own place in the group takes time and may be intimidating. Different people will react in different ways to new group members. Some colleagues will be looking for you to prove yourself in a particular way; others may offer help and support; others may seem indifferent. Some may even feel threatened.

Veteran teachers will give you advice which will be communicated in a variety of different styles. You will view some of the advice as being positive and supportive. Other advice will feel critical. It is important to try to respond in a professional manner. Reserve judgment until you have a better understanding of the environment, the culture, and the individuals who are part of your school community. You will be wise to do a great deal of listening: think twice before commenting on what you observe, and be careful not to gossip or talk to teachers about other teachers.

Think carefully about what constitutes a professional relationship. In a professional relationship one separates one's feelings, likes and dislikes, and emotional responses from one's goals. To keep your goals as a teacher paramount you must let go of pride, hurt feelings, and vulnerability to insult. Keep in mind that your first impressions of a person may turn out to be misleading. A professional sees beyond personalities and types; a professional teacher sees the value in building relationships with a variety of people in order to meet common goals.

It is also helpful to remember that teachers are at different stages in their own professional development and in their own personal lives, and they are responding from their own particular situations or stages of development. Your colleagues may be involved in major professional commitments, such as being a teacher leader for a new literacy project, writing an article for publication, organizing a major conference for a professional network of math teachers, working on the math/science frameworks for their system, serving as a union officer, or finishing a Master's degree program. They may have limited time for other activities. Teachers may also have personal and family commitments that are time consuming and drain their energy for a given time period: a teacher may have a new baby at home, may be caring for an aging parent, may be recovering from a recent illness, or may have a second job. Although they may typically like to interact with new teachers, they may not have time to do so during the current school year. They may be more available at other times of their teaching careers. You may also encounter a small group of teachers who are discontent with the profession and are waiting to retire. They may try to draw you into their negativity about the school and about teaching. Certainly, there are issues to critique in every teaching situation and rarely will you encounter an organization that functions perfectly. However, you might want to be wary of colleagues who consistently choose a negative stance. They can consume your time, drain your energy, and add little that is constructive.

If you are a student teacher, you may feel that you aren't getting enough guidance and feedback from your cooperating teacher. It is important that you are sensitive to her needs as a person. Although you may ask for the help you need, do so in a way that demonstrates empathy for her professional and life situation. Work with your teacher and college supervisor to figure out how to build in time for regular feedback.

You will find that different colleagues can offer different kinds of support — from a fleeting conversation or social exchange to being an ongoing resource on substantive issues of teaching; from expertise in a particular subject area to extensive knowledge of classroom management strategies; from an active involvement in community agencies and resources to an exceptional sense of how to design a classroom environment. Even those colleagues who do not seem to be in the same philosophical camp as you may have much to offer you. A second year teacher explains,

> My first year of teaching junior high school, I shared a homeroom with a veteran teacher who had a very different philosophy of education. We tended to organize the room differently—he liked the chairs arranged in rows and liked to teach the whole class together. I engaged in frequent group work and liked to group the desks in blocks of four or five. He used a lot of worksheets and followed a textbook closely. I often brought in hands-on materials as part of my lessons, used cooperative learning groups, and tried to engage students in small group discussions. Yet, he knew individual students quite well and was excellent in managing large groups. He understood that students needed structure and predictability. At first, we argued about the room arrangement and about our approaches to teaching. I didn't know how I was going to co-exist with this colleague for a whole school year! Much to my surprise, as we got to know each other and to trust each other, I found that I actually could learn from my colleague. We were able to eventually joke about our differences. I learned a great deal from my colleague about individual students and about how to provide consistency in structure and procedures, even though I was operating out of a different frame of reference regarding approaches to teaching. I also like to think that he may have learned something from me during that year.

Veteran teachers sometimes complain that student teachers and beginning teachers are too idealistic, have "pie in the sky ideas," and do not understand the context in which they are teaching. They report that new teachers are too quick to judge them on superficial grounds. Try to keep an open mind. If you are perceived as being judgmental you will not benefit from the wisdom of some of your colleagues. As was pointed out in Chapter Two, it is important to hang onto your ideals and to work out your own teaching style. Proceed cautiously, without alienating colleagues who share other perspectives on teaching. Your ideas may be more readily accepted once you gain the support of your colleagues. One beginning teacher, in reminiscing about her first year, commented,

> Some teaching practices did not seem right to me. I had to be very careful about whom I asked questions of. I found a veteran teacher who was very helpful and cautioned me about raising these questions in grade level meetings. It was wise advice in this particular situation and kind of her to let me know. By the end of the year, after the district had mandated new directives regarding the reading curriculum, several experienced teachers asked me if I would share some of my strategies for teaching reading and my language arts materials. I was totally surprised and flattered that experienced teachers were seeking me out for advice. I think the cautiousness I exercised during the year paid off.

A principal in an elementary school observed some of his beginning teachers exclaiming the first month of school, "I would never do things that way!" By the third month of school they were asking their colleagues, "How do you do that?"

MENTORING

A more formalized way of gaining support is working with a mentor. When you begin your first year of teaching, you may find that you have been matched with a veteran teacher who is to be your "mentor." In some states, mentoring is a component of a required induction year program. Sometimes a college and school system will develop a mentoring program together. These programs may consist of training for the mentors, an orientation for mentors and mentees, mentor/mentee meetings, and a series of workshops or classes offered throughout the year. In some programs, release time is provided to facilitate mentors and mentees meeting together . Other programs are more informal and may not provide much structure and support beyond an initial orientation and a few follow-up meetings. In situations where no formal mentor program exists, a veteran teacher may generously offer to help a beginning teacher and may serve as an informal mentor, sharing materials, helping solve problems, coaching, supporting, and playing many of the roles of a formal mentor.

"In what ways can a mentor help me?" is a question you may ask as a new teacher. A mentor or an experienced teacher can offer many "different kinds of assistance with varying degrees of directness" (Wildman, Magliaro, Niles & Niles, 1992, p.207). One way that a mentor can support you is to encourage you to reflect on your teaching practices and to select the practices that best fit the situation you are confronting. The mentor might help you broaden your perspective by working with you to generate a range of possible solutions to a problem or issue, some of which you as a beginning teacher may not have in your repertoire to consider. Mentors may also be directive and give you specific advice for dealing with a situation, for example, how to set up a work folder for substitutes, how to deal with a particular type of family issue, how to structure a Back-to-School Night, or how to order books and supplies. Mentors can help you with instructional issues, with planning lessons and units, designing worksheets, structuring cooperative learning groups, and advising you on strategies for approaching certain types of behavioral issues. Mentors can model teaching practices and can engage in collaborative planning. Mentors can also observe you teaching and give you feedback on their observations. Three beginning teachers describe the ways in which their mentors supported them.

> I couldn't have survived my first year of teaching without my mentor. There is so much unwritten and unspoken information I never would have known. Nobody told me that every teacher wrote regular newsletters to their students' families. Nobody schooled me in how to organize a field trip and advised me that teachers often buddied up to lessen the cost of renting the bus. Nobody informed me that you could submit a request to attend a professional development conference outside of the system. Nobody advised me that the librarian welcomed collaborations with classroom teachers and often helped teachers plan interdisciplinary curriculum units. I also did not know that the librarian had a software budget and that teachers could request that she order software that they could use in their classrooms. My list goes on and on.

> My mentor helped me generate solutions to problems. I would describe a teaching dilemma to her. We would then generate several possible solutions. My mentor often shared solutions she and other colleagues developed for solving similar dilemmas. We would then select one solution and I would try it. We would meet again to evaluate and discuss the outcome of the strategy I had tried. If necessary, we tried several different solutions.

> I needed to have tunnel vision my first year of teaching and found that I

had to focus on basics. I knew my content area well, but that was not the issue. I needed to develop systems, routines, and structures, and to learn to be consistent in my implementation. Kids feel more secure in my classroom when I have systems and structures in place. I needed to work on structuring my lessons, on strategies for preparing my students for transitions within the lesson, on incorporating adaptations for specific students, and on ideas for students who finished their work early. I spent focused time with my mentor working on these issues. My mentor let me observe her, and she did a lot of modeling for me. I could not have maintained my tunnel vision without the help of my mentor.

If you find yourself in a situation where you have been assigned a mentor, try to use the relationship to its fullest. Hopefully your mentor will be a teacher who is teaching at your grade level and who is located in your building. Spend time getting to know your mentor and building a relationship. Of course it is ideal if you and your mentor share a common philosophy of teaching and are compatible personalities. Even if this is not the case, a mentor teacher has much to offer a new teacher, such as:

- ❏ help with problem solving,
- ❏ information about school policies and procedures,
- ❏ explanation of the unwritten policies,
- ❏ sharing of resources,
- ❏ information about working with families,
- ❏ help with time management and planning,
- ❏ alternative ways of thinking about classroom management,
- ❏ tips on how to organize administrative tasks,
- ❏ explanation of roles of school specialists
- ❏ information relating to curriculum,
- ❏ insights into the wider school culture,
- ❏ information about the community.

A mentor teacher can help explain aspects of the school culture, can advocate for you as a new teacher and can give you emotional and personal support as a new professional entering a complex profession. Some mentors may also be well networked beyond the school system and may be active participants in professional organizations to which they can introduce you.

Although not every mentor/mentee relationship is a perfect match, it is useful to build as positive a relationship as possible and work from the strengths that your mentor has to offer. Similarly, not all of the workshops and support groups offered by your system as part of the induction program will be equally rewarding, but your participation can be important to you. Try to be open to the opportunities presented. At the very least, you will meet other new teachers who are struggling with the same issues as you are, and you will meet some veteran teachers who will be wonderful colleagues to you throughout your career. You will begin to learn how to be a supportive colleague yourself. By working with others in various groups and individually, an induction program will force you to leave your classroom and to join others in discussing issues of teaching.

If you find that you and your mentor are not congenial, and you have tried to work in a positive mode, you may need to find support through informal structures. There are still areas in which you can learn from your mentor, but you may not feel the trust or rapport to share some of the important issues you are confronting. You may get advice that seems didactic and seems to say, "This is the only way to do things." You may have a mentor who does not have much time to spend with you because the school does not give mentors release time, and the mentor has too many other responsibilities. You may have a mentor who does not want to appear intrusive, and you may have to take the initiative in scheduling meetings. You may have a mentor whose philosophy of teaching is not compatible with yours. This is a wonderful opportunity to practice your new professionalism. To whatever extent possible, try to use the mentoring relationship to your advantage.

OTHER ADULT TO ADULT RELATIONSHIPS

You will have many opportunities to work closely with colleagues in schools today. Adult to adult interactions are increasingly important features of schools, yet working with other adults is not necessarily emphasized in teacher training programs and student teaching placements. The focus in these programs is primarily on adult interactions with children. As you begin to teach, you will want to be more cognizant of the set of adult relationships in which you are involved.

As a beginning teacher, you may find that you have other adults working directly with you in your classroom. You may be supervising a classroom assistant; working with a reading paraprofessional who spends two to three hours a day providing services to students in a reading center in a corner of your classroom; or you may be collaborating or co-teaching with a special education inclusion teacher who works with small groups of children in your class. In addition, many specialists may be delivering services to students in your class. These might include occupational therapists, physical therapists, speech and language teachers, special educators, reading specialists, guidance counselors, and expressive therapists. Your students also probably attend art, physical education, music, technology, and/or library classes during scheduled periods of the week and work with teachers trained in these specialties.

These services may reflect several different service delivery models:

❏ subjects delivered to your whole class in the specialist's classroom (gym, art room, music room);

❏ services delivered directly to a small group of students in your classroom;

❏ services in which individual students or groups of students may be pulled out of your classroom at specified times;

❏ consultative services in which specialists advise you on how to integrate specific strategies, techniques, or adapted curriculum within the general education classroom;

❏ services that involve a specialist who is co-teaching with you.

Since some school systems are in transition in defining how special education services are delivered, different models can exist simultaneously in the same school. Formal and informal models may vary greatly, and the implementation of these models may depend on the personal relationships of the collaborating teachers.

All of these colleagues will bring perspectives from their own professional training and practice as well as a particular philosophy of education. Some of the relationships will be predefined, and role responsibilities will be clear. Other relationships will be less clearly defined and will need to be carefully worked out together. Your colleagues will have many different styles of working: some will welcome collaboration and will engage in joint goal setting and problem solving; others will be operating from a consultative model in which they will be sharing their expertise; others may be working quite autonomously in their particular specialty and see little need for teaming or collaboration.

These relationships will be structured in different ways also. In some you will be a colleague reporting to the same principal. In others you may be in a direct supervisory role. In some cases, the personnel working in your classroom (for example, an aide or reading assistant) may report to another supervisor such as the district's reading or special education director or director of pupil personnel. In some of these relationships an individual may not even have a direct reporting relationship to the principal of your school and may report solely to the district's director of special education or reading. Understanding the structure of these role relationships will help you in the communication process, will give you deeper insight into issues that may arise, and will ultimately strengthen the kinds of services you can offer your students.

NEW TEACHER AS SUPERVISOR

In many schools today, you, as a beginning teacher, may have a classroom assistant working in your room for part of the day. There are many types of people who become assistants. The classroom assistant may have worked in the school for several years and may live in the community. She may be twenty years older than you, may have her own family, and be very familiar with parenting issues. She may be a recently certified teacher who didn't find, or has not chosen to work in, a fulltime teaching position. You and your assistant may be from different cultural backgrounds and may have different values, different conceptions of the role of a teacher, and different cultural perspectives. You can learn a great deal from your assistant. Yet you are her supervisor, and you must be prepared for this role.

One veteran teacher advises new teachers to take the necessary time in the beginning of the year to meet with classroom assistants to articulate your expectations, to define your roles, and to describe how you will work together. It is important for you and your assistant to be clear on the formal and informal job description, as suggested by the questions below.

❏ Is your assistant supporting you administratively and helping with copying, preparing materials, classroom set-up and organization?
❏ Is your assistant helping students transition from specials to the classroom?
❏ Is your assistant overseeing lunch or recess?
❏ Does your assistant have teaching responsibilities? If so, what are they and what are your expectations?

❏ Is your assistant responsible for supporting an individual student or a group of students in your classroom?

You will also want to set aside time each week to plan together, to reflect on the events of the week, and to set goals for and share information regarding individual students.

It is critical that your assistant understand your educational philosophy, your teaching style, your expectations for classroom management, and your classroom routines. You, in turn, need to understand your assistant's educational philosophy and views on classroom management so you can work out your differences. Differences in style and perspectives can enrich the classroom experience for your students, as long as you figure out the areas in which consistency is needed. Teaming with an assistant can be immensely rewarding for both of you and for your students. You need to spend the time and take the initiative to make this relationship a productive one. The vignettes below will highlight some of the dilemmas you may face in working with a classroom assistant and will help you think of ways to prepare for this new role.

6.2 Exercise for Your Journal: Sharing My Classroom

One classroom teacher describes a dilemma she faces in working with a reading assistant. A reading assistant reports to the district literacy coordinator and spends three hours each day in my classroom working with individual students who need support in reading and language arts. The assistant has set up a corner in my room in which she provides her tutoring. Last year I developed language arts centers and book groups and wanted the reading specialist to work with several of the students in the context of the groups and centers. When I talked to the reading assistant, she told me that the literacy coordinator had instructed her to provide individual tutoring.

- What advice would you give this classroom teacher? How should she proceed? Whom should she involve in the discussion of this issue?
- What are some possible outcomes?
- Write the approaches you develop in your journal.

6.3 Exercise for Your Journal: How Do I Give Negative Feedback?

My classroom assistant works in my room four hours a day. She is well intentioned and cares about the students but does not always communicate in a positive way with them. She sometimes makes negative statements when she is feeling stressed. This response makes students angry and unable to address situations that are being brought to their attention. Recently a parent called and complained about the way my assistant was talking to her son. I know I have to give this feedback to my assistant and establish a way for us to work on this issue together. I find this difficult to do. Write in your journal answers to the following questions.

- What can you do to improve the situation?
- What are important points to discuss with your classroom aide? How will you discuss some of the sensitive issues in this situation?
- How will you work together in the future? What kind of supervision or leadership will you provide?
- What kind of forums for ongoing communication will you establish?
- What will you say to the parent?
- To whom can you turn to for support?

6.4 Exercise for Your Journal: Observations from a Student Teacher's Perspective

If you are a student teacher, and there is a classroom assistant working in the class, what can you learn about working with a classroom aide? How will you work together with the assistant and the cooperating teacher? What issues, if any, have arisen for you due to this teaming situation? Have you discussed these with your cooperating teacher or supervisor? This is an opportunity to practice teaming skills and to observe the teacher's supervisory skills. Observe the relationship between the assistant and the classroom teacher, think about the following questions, and record your observations in your journal. Discuss them in your seminar or with another student teacher.

- How does the teacher use the classroom assistant?
- Does the assistant play an active instructional role in the classroom?
- How effectively do they communicate? Are they consistent in their messages to students and parents?
- What mechanisms do they have in place for planning?
- How do they work out issues that arise?
- What have you learned about working with a classroom assistant?

COLLEGIAL MODELS

Co-Teaching

Co-teaching, which evolved from the team teaching models of the sixties, (Bair & Woodward, as cited in Reinhiller, 1996) can be defined as occurring when "two or more professionals jointly deliver substantive instruction to a diverse, or blended, group of students in a single, physical space"(Friend & Cook, 1996, p. 45). Co-teaching is most frequently used today in inclusive settings in which a general education and special education teacher jointly plan and teach a group of students in a single classroom. Co-teaching models vary; Marilyn Friend and Lynne Cook (1996) describe five approaches to co-teaching:

1. One teaching, one supporting: One teacher is in charge, and the other teacher observes and provides assistance to individual students.

2. Station teaching: Teachers divide the content and each teaches a segment and the students rotate in a small group to each teacher's station.

3. Parallel teaching: The teachers jointly plan the lesson, and each teacher works with half of the class, teaching the same content.

4. Alternative teaching: One teacher provides a different approach to a small group, while the other teacher teaches the larger group.

5. Team teaching: Both teachers are responsible for instruction throughout the lesson, but may teach different portions of the lesson or use different types of instruction.

Co-teaching is also sometimes referred to as collaborative teaching and each of the different approaches involve some level of collaborative activity such as joint planning, decision making, problem solving and ongoing communication. These activities require flexibility, the building of trusting relationships, and the willingness to talk through issues and conflicts. Friend and Cook (1996) have developed a framework for assessing co-teaching readiness, as well as a set of questions to discuss with your co-teaching partner that help you make explicit your philosophies, beliefs, and teaching styles. Co-teaching seems to work best when assignments are voluntary and when teachers work together effectively as a team. When these conditions are in place, teachers frequently report personal and professional growth, as well as academic growth in their students. However, when the chemistry is not present, when one of the parties does not want to co-teach, when there is no real parity in the relationship, negative effects are often reported (Budoff, 1999, chap. 8). A teacher in a new teacher support group consistently reported,

> The match is not there. My co-teacher has taught for fifteen years and sees the classroom as her territory and views me as a special education assistant. Even though my supervisor is supporting me, my role is limited, and I cannot give the level of academic support that the students should be receiving.

Opportunities to co-teach often make themselves available as part of the student teaching experience. Learn to recognize these opportunities and take advantage of them. Some cooperating teachers suggest to their student teachers that they co-teach a particular lesson or unit with them. Student teachers may also co-teach a lesson or unit with another student teacher or student intern. This experience has often been an invaluable way of building in opportunities for reflection in the planning, implementation, and evaluation of the lesson and of experiencing a lesson being taught from multiple perspectives.

As a student teacher, think about ways you can work with your college supervisor, cooperating teacher, and other student teachers to build in opportunities to co-teach. Two student teachers could jointly plan one lesson and co-teach it in two different classes at the same grade level, at two different grade levels, or to two different groups in the same classroom. The partners might be two student teachers in a practicum placement or one in a pre-practicum and one in a practicum. Student teachers in general education and special education might co-teach a lesson in a general education classroom.

Peer Coaching

Another model that teachers are using for ongoing reflection and feedback on their teaching is that of peer coaching. In most peer coaching models, a teacher will identify an area or aspect of her teaching that she would like her partner or team members to observe. Usually a pre-conference is scheduled, and the teacher identifies what she wants her peer coach(es) to focus on — for example, questioning strategies, adaptations of a lesson for students who have identified special needs, facilitation of group discussions, or transitioning students from whole group to small group instruction. Her partner or team members observe her teaching the lesson. After the lesson, a post-conference is held, and the teachers observing give feedback and engage in a conversation regarding their observations. A rich conversation regarding issues of teaching usually ensues, and all of the teachers usually learn from the observation. The teacher who has been observed may then take the feedback and her own reflections and apply them to her work, making changes in a lesson or being more self-aware of an aspect of her own teaching. During the course of the year, the pairs or teams of teachers have multiple opportunities to observe one another. This opportunity gives teachers a chance to see how other professionals approach similar challenges of teaching.

Some schools have set aside time for teachers to engage in this process of observation and reflection with peers. In one school, the principal facilitates the process by planning coverage for the teachers so that they can easily leave their classrooms to observe others. Many teachers who have engaged in this process have found it enormously helpful. It enables them to grow as teachers in areas they have identified, engenders renewed respect for their colleagues, and makes their future conversations richer because they have a better understanding of each other's teaching styles and particular classroom contexts. Peer coaching builds respect and trust amongst colleagues, which makes it easier to routinely turn to one another for help and advice. It is a practice directly related to student learning that can encourage risk taking and continuous learning for teachers.

Peer coaching can be a wonderful tool for the student teacher. Even if not formalized, student teachers can find a buddy and can go through the process of peer coaching together. Sometimes it is helpful to engage in peer coaching at the earliest stages of teaching and to obtain feedback from other student teachers as well as from a supervisor or veteran teacher. Some of the beginning teacher issues, which may be internalized parts of a veteran teacher's repertoire, resonate more for someone at the same beginning stage of teaching. Peer coaching is also a way to practice giving and receiving feedback, can help you build good collegial habits in the early stages of your career, and help you support your specific professional development needs and goals.

School-Based Teams

Although teachers often talk about teacher isolation, there are many opportunities to participate on teams in schools, and these teams may provide access to colleagues with whom you may not ordinarily come in frequent contact and who may be potential collaborators. Most of these teams have regular meetings throughout the year, consistent membership, and some shared goals. The most common types of teams are described below.

Grade Level Teams: Teachers from one grade level meet on a regular basis to discuss curriculum and assessment tools for the particular grade level, discuss individual students, design units of study, share resources, and meet with specialists.

Cluster Teams: Teachers from several grade levels (for example, K-3, 4-6, 7-8) meet on a regular basis to discuss curriculum and assessment, design units of study, share resources, meet with specialists, coordinate curriculum at different grade levels, and work on schoolwide issues. For example, a cluster group may draft a new conferencing form, review its literacy program, inventory its math materials, or design activities for an upcoming professional development event.

Departments: Teachers who teach the same discipline on the middle school or secondary level meet to coordinate work across grade levels, to plan curriculum, order materials, and discuss assessment tools and teaching strategies.

House Teams or Interdisciplinary Teams: A group of 5-8 middle or high school teachers work with the same 80-120 students. Teachers meet on a regular basis to develop curriculum or to collaborate on interdisciplinary units; discuss the progress of individual students; and plan field trips, special events, or an evening open house or parent conferences.

Student Support Teams or Student Assistance Teams: Teams include teacher representatives; school specialists, such as guidance counselor, special educator, speech and language therapist, nurse, parent liaison; and representatives from community agencies that provide services to the school, such as a community counseling center or health center. Teachers volunteer to give a presentation of a child that is having difficulty in class. The team makes recommendations to the teacher for supporting the student and the student's family.

Pre-referral Teams: If a teacher suspects that a student may need to be referred for special education services, the teacher will present the student to a pre-referral team. The pre-referral team consists of the classroom teacher and school specialists, such as the special education teacher, speech therapist, guidance counselor. The team makes recommendations for ways the teacher can support the student in the classroom. The teacher implements the recommendations for a period of time. The team reevaluates the student and recommends a referral to special education or recommends that the student continue to be supported in the regular classroom.

Special Education Evaluation Team: The formal, multidisciplinary evaluation team assesses and evaluates a student's eligibility for special education services and writes an Individualized Education Program. The team has an annual meeting for each student on an educational plan to evaluate the student's progress and to update the plan. Teams consist of the parents or guardians of the student referred, the student (depending on age), classroom teacher, special education chairperson, and the appropriate specialists involved with the individual student.

Professional Development School (PDS) Teams: If your school is part of a professional development school partnership with a local college or university, there may be a PDS team that meets regularly to plan activities for the partnership. Some PDS partnerships have governance teams or a school based team that meets regularly. Since one of the goals of most professional school partnerships is to enhance the professional development of college and school faculty, these teams may be a good way to find collegial support and to work with colleagues in a particular area you are interested in developing in your teaching.

School Governance Teams or School Councils: In some states, site-based management or school councils are mandated as part of educational reform. Some school councils are connected with reform models in which a school governance team is an integral part of the model. Governance teams usually represent all the school's constituencies—administration, teachers, specialists, paraprofessionals, students, parents, and community groups. School governance teams review many aspects of schooling including school budgets, curricular and assessment issues, building safety and climate, parental involvement; they often serve as advisory groups to the principal. Some school systems provide formal training for their governance teams in group decision making, school budgeting, and curricular issues. School council meetings are open to the school community, and agendas and minutes are usually available. You may not have time to serve on the team as a first year teacher, but it may be of interest to you the second or third year of your career. During your beginning years of teaching, you may want to observe a school council meeting or keep updated on the issues the council is addressing.

Teacher Teams for Implementing Change: These teams are often part of grants for staff development, and they focus on a particular subject area. As part of the grant, a team of teachers is trained in a particular curricular innovation, and they in turn become teacher leaders in their school for the implementation of the new initiative. The team often meets on a regular basis for one to three years or for the duration of the grant.

Some of the teaming situations may be required — grade level meetings, cluster meetings, meetings with the special education evaluation team — and others may be available as a resource — child study team or a school team that is providing leadership for a specific innovation. You will find teams that work well together — that have clear goals, effective group processes, and strong leadership. Some of the teams may discuss issues that dovetail perfectly with your own professional needs at the time. Other agendas may seem important but peripheral to what you can manage as a new teacher.

Not all of these teams may live up to your hopes and expectations. In some situations, team goals may not be clearly defined and/or there is too much to accomplish in an unrealistic timeframe. For example, some grade level teams meet once a week for a class period of 50 minutes. The time is not always protected and by the time all members arrive, 10 or 15 minutes may have elapsed. Team members may have multiple agendas, from coordinating logistical issues to discussing individual students to designing curriculum. There may be little follow-up from week to week of issues discussed. In some situations you will find that team members do not want to be team players and have no intention of collaborating. These meetings may not always seem to be of immediate value, and you may have many pressing tasks to accomplish in your own classroom. Try to view the meetings as opportunities. Use these meetings as a forum to get to know your colleagues in another context and you may, over the course of time, find group members who are compatible and are interested in working with you. You may also be able to eventually influence the agenda for the meeting and help focus the meetings.

Aside from the regular teams described above, your school and school district will have ad hoc committees that are formed to accomplish a particular purpose. There may be a committee to redesign the system's professional development programs, a committee to reevaluate report cards in the elementary grades, or a committee within your school to plan the Author's Week programs. As a beginning teacher, you have a full plate, and you will want to carefully pick and choose additional commitments. You may decide that it is not a good idea to take on any extra responsibility your first year. On the other hand, you may decide that committee work is an excellent way to become involved with colleagues, and you might consider participating in a committee during your second semester. Try to volunteer for activities that have clearly defined tasks and timelines. Even if you do not participate, it is helpful to be aware of the various opportunities. Think about how you could fit some committee work into your schedule the following year, or think about participating in a summer institute or curricular initiative sponsored by your district. The ability to become an institutional player and to work with a variety of teachers across your district will provide you with new colleagues, a wide range of perspectives, and varied opportunities to support your continuous learning and professional development.

Collaborative Approaches to Curriculum Planning and Evaluation

In recent years we've become aware of new approaches to working collaboratively with colleagues to improve teaching practices. The two which we would like to mention here are the lesson study and collaborative examination of students' work. The lesson study, based on a Japanese model, involves a group of teachers working together on the development of a lesson plan or research lesson. The research lesson is presented by one of the teachers who is observed by the rest of the group. The lesson is then critically analyzed by the group of teachers observing (Watanabe, 2002). Observers may be assigned specific areas of focus or specific observation tasks, such as watching the responses of an individual student or listening and recording conversations of one of the groups of students. An essential component of the research lesson is the "post lesson discussion" by the group of teachers who observed the lesson. "Unlike classroom observation as it is traditionally practiced in the U. S., the focus is primarily on the lesson itself, not the teacher and her or his technique. The lesson is then revised, taught and observed again" (Kelly, 2002, p. 5). Lesson study can be applied to a variety of content areas. Some of the perceived benefits of lesson study include a breakdown of teacher isolation and the creation of a process in which teachers are trained to ask for help. It enables participants to acquire fresh approaches and ideas and to strengthen content area knowledge (Kelly, 2002; Watanabe, 2002).

Another collaborative approach involves teachers working together as a group to look at and analyze student work. "This type of reflective practice is becoming more common in schools today as schools strive for more public and widely understood linkages between standards, learning tasks, and assessments" (Fleming, 2000). A group of educators in a school system might meet to examine student writing across the primary grades. After looking at samples of student work, they develop rubrics for assessing particular writing skills. These rubrics are based on the school system's or state's standards and the student writing samples that were examined. A group of "critical friends" might meet regularly during the year to examine "student work and the teacher work that prompted it" (Bambino, 2002). The group develops a format for reflection and discussion of student work. Members may present a particular assignment, the accompanying rubric, and their students' work. The group asks questions, makes observations, and the presenting teacher takes notes and chooses ideas to adopt from the discussion.

DEALING WITH CONFLICTS

In all relationships, conflict is inevitable and as a teacher, even with the best working relationships, you will experience conflicts with others. Part of your professional training undoubtedly focused on the mediation of conflict at school with children. But what thought have you given to the possible conflicts between you and other teachers? Sometimes veteran teachers are quick to judge the new ideas and boundless energy of a young first year teacher. What will you do when someone with many years of teaching experience disagrees with your teaching philosophy and tries to undermine your efforts by commenting negatively about the way you conduct your class? What will you do when you see someone handling a situation with a student in a way that is contrary to your own beliefs? What do you do when colleagues hoard materials that you desperately need? Being aware of some of the typical conflicts that can arise in school settings, understanding your own attitudes toward conflict, and understanding how conflict is dealt with in your school culture will better prepare you to work collaboratively with colleagues.

Conflict is not necessarily bad. Conflict may result in growth for the parties involved, and schools that actively address conflicts may be healthy institutions in which to work. Attitudes toward conflict may be culturally based, and norms regarding conflict may differ among families or between females or males within a given culture. The assumptions we make about conflict are based on experiences and interpretations that are an unconscious part of us. We experience and respond to conflict daily.

We have a set of internal norms that tell us what is appropriate and what is not. Assume that these norms are not the same for many of the adults and children in the school community where you work. What will you do when a conflict arises? What do you know about your own feelings about conflict? Can you articulate them? If so, how will they serve you in the school community? As you become clearer about your own assumptions, you can begin to try to understand responses from others. Some cultures sanction and value conflict as a way of communicating and working out difference. Other cultures or subcultures condemn conflict and require avoidance at all costs. Be assured that during your teaching career, you will meet people from both kinds of cultures and many in-between. By looking at conflict from many points of view, you will have a better chance of creatively responding to conflict and learning and growing from the experience.

6.5 Exercise for Your Journal:
    Identifying Your Personal Approach to Conflict
    and Your School's Approach to Conflict

A first step for you to take in thinking about how you may approach conflict in the workplace is to examine your experiences, reactions, and assumptions about the nature and purpose of conflict. Ponder your experiences growing up and during your years in college.

- What were you taught by your family about conflict, aggressive behavior and the resolution of conflict?
- What did you learn from your experiences with peers and your formal training in college?
- Do you feel comfortable disagreeing with someone who is more experienced and more knowledgeable?
- Do you fear conflict or even the possibility of conflict? Or do you welcome it?
- Do you try to avoid conflict at all costs?

Answering these questions will help you begin to understand yourself better and mediate some of your responses, even those responses that you feel are automatic and outside of your control. According to Webb and Sherman (1989), "much of what we learn from culture becomes taken for granted and sinks below the level of conscious reflection." We need to make our "taken-for-granted assumptions retrievable, understandable, and when necessary changeable" (p. 64). This is especially true for conflict and conflict resolution.

A second step is to observe in your school and try to get an understanding of how conflict is dealt with in your particular school setting. Take notes in your journal and try to answer the questions that follow.

- Are there forums for discussing issues, for working out disagreements and for group problem solving?

- Are conflicts usually swept under the rug and not addressed directly?
- How are philosophical differences among the staff addressed? Is there agreement to disagree?
- Think about an example of a conflict you have witnessed in your school setting. How was it dealt with? Was it addressed directly? Was it resolved?
- Does the district or school offer teachers training in conflict resolution?
- Interview two veteran teachers and ask them how they view conflict resolution in your school setting.

Once you have a better understanding of your own personal style in dealing with conflict and of how conflict is addressed in your particular school setting, you will be more aware of how you want to respond when you find yourself in a disagreement with a colleague. There are no easy answers, and you may have different ways of responding to different individuals and different types of conflicts. In some cases, you may decide that the best approach is not to respond. However, being aware of issues around conflict can give you the appropriate distance to choose an approach that works for you in your particular school setting. This professional distance may help you deal with your anger if you decide it is not beneficial to try to resolve the conflict.

You may have a set of personal strategies that you find useful for dealing with conflict, or you may decide that it will be helpful to enroll in an inservice training or workshop on conflict resolution in order to learn some specific skills that you can apply. Finding a model or a set of strategies that match your personal style and beliefs may make you more confident when you find yourself in situations involving conflict.

HOW TO BE A GOOD COLLEAGUE

You may feel that, being a beginning teacher, you have little to offer your colleagues. However, you can begin to form positive, collegial habits even if you feel like you are in need of a great deal of professional support yourself. Taking advantage of multiple opportunities to get to know your colleagues, both personally and professionally, through staff meetings, in-service training, team meetings, bus duty, school related social occasions or casual conversations in the teacher's room or hallways, will help you build a pool of potential collaborators. As we have discussed in this chapter, asking for assistance and help and being open to constructive criticism are essential to your initial growth, and are positive habits to cultivate throughout your teaching career. Engage in professional sharing whenever possible — invite a colleague to observe a lesson in your classroom, look at student work with another teacher, critique a unit of study with teachers at your grade level. You may not have time during your first year of teaching to join a study group or yearlong learning team, but find some time to talk about your teaching practices with your colleagues. You will find these discussions and exchanges energizing.

If you are receiving support from a mentor, you will have contributions to make in return. You are giving the mentor an opportunity to discuss teaching practices, to think through challenging situations and view them from a different perspective, and to learn about some of the new research or approaches that you have recently studied in your teacher preparation program. You can begin to develop the habit of sharing your own knowledge and resources.

View yourself as an institutional player and not just as a "second grade teacher" or "a special education teacher." Even if you need to spend the majority of time focusing on your classroom and students and your own first year teaching struggles, become aware of school wide and district issues and initiatives. If you develop strong working relationships with a small group of teachers or specialists at your grade level or in your subject area, continue to find ways to relate to the wider group of teachers in your school. Part of your work as a teacher is upholding standards and developing curricular coherence throughout the grade levels and working for improvements in your school as a whole (Fullan & Hargreaves, 1996).

SUMMARY

Finding colleagues who can become allies and give you support during the critical first years of teaching is of great importance to you as a beginning teacher. You may find this support in a variety of places — through a formal or informal mentoring relationship, help and assistance from grade level teachers or an interdisciplinary team, a specialist with whom you form a partnership, or a group of beginning teachers in your school. If it is difficult to find this support within your school, try some of the networks described in Chapter Nine.

Suggested Resources

Bolton, R. (1979). *People skills: How to assert yourself, listen to others, and resolve conflicts.* New York: Simon & Schuster.

Friend, M. & Cook, L. (1996). *Interactions: Collaboration skills for school professionals (2nd ed.).* White Plains, New York: Longman Publishers.

Fullan, M. & Hargreaves, A. (1996). *What's worth fighting for in your school.* New York: Teachers College Press.

Maeroff, G. (1993). *Team building for school change: Equipping teachers for new roles.* New York: Teacher's College Press.

CHAPTER SEVEN

REFLECTING ON YOUR PRACTICE

> *Reflection is a gift we give ourselves, not passive thought*
> *that lolls aimlessly in our minds, but an effort we must*
> *approach with rigor, with some purpose in mind, and in*
> *some formal way, so as to reveal the wisdom embedded in*
> *our experience. Through reflection, we develop context spe-*
> *cific theories that further our own understanding of our*
> *work and generate knowledge to inform future practice.*
> (Killion & Todnem, 1991, p.14)

While engaging in the day to day activities of teaching, you'll have both successes and challenges daily. You may feel as though you're reeling through space with no time to stop and think about anything. The reality is that time is a major issue for all new teachers. It's tempting, and sometimes necessary, to move from one activity to the next, or one day to the next, seemingly without reflecting on the meaning of what happened during the last activity or the previous day. However, in order to understand all that is occurring in your classroom, in order to learn from your successes and mistakes, it is necessary to stop, to think, to reflect. Reflection is an important habit to develop because over the course of your teaching career, you can only improve your teaching practice by thinking about your teaching, evaluating its effectiveness, and carefully considering what you might do differently. There are many different strategies for facilitating reflection. In this chapter, we will attempt to provide guidance on ways to do this constructively, without becoming overwhelmed.

As we were writing this book, we asked a sample of teachers how they're able to reflect on their teaching. We interviewed new teachers, veteran teachers, general education and special education teachers, from both elementary and middle schools in urban and suburban school districts. They recognized the need for reflection and have found strategies to make it happen. These were some of the ways in which they've learned to reflect on their work:

- ◆ "I make time in the morning before class. I think about how I want the day to go."

- ◆ "At the end of the day I spend 15 minutes evaluating how I think the day went."

- ◆ "I share my ideas and thoughts with my co-teacher throughout the day."

- ◆ "I look during the activity to make sure that different children are engaged. I need to reach all these kids at all their different levels. I need to make sure that all students are feeling successful."

- ◆ "I watch for distractibility. Some of that is classroom management, but when students are not paying attention it is a good indicator that the lesson is not working."

- ◆ "I am constantly reevaluating during the day."

- ◆ "I meet with colleagues on a regular basis, attend summer institutes, and read in my field."

- ◆ "Prior to teaching a lesson, I think about what can happen. During the lesson, I ask myself how they are reacting. Afterwards, I ask how did it go?"

- ◆ "I use my planbook to write goals. I make notes of what I missed and when something went well."

- ◆ "I always reflect on my teaching. I ask myself how was my approach, how was my presentation (visual and verbal), and what can I do to improve?"

- ◆ "I evaluate each lesson. I ask did students meet their goals, did I use their learning styles? I think about ways to get students there. I'm conscious of being a facilitator or lecturer. I ask myself if I asked the questions well. I continue my professional growth through professional collaboration and courses."

These strategies seem to work for the individuals who use them. As you move from the role of student to the role of professional educator, you'll need to move beyond reliance on your professors' ideas and opinions towards incorporating what you've learned in your preparation program into your own professional ideas and practices. Reflecting on your own teaching in a thoughtful way will help you to do this. All that you have learned must be integrated into your own teaching style and personality and applied to the particular context, community, and classroom in which you find yourself. Setting your own professional goals and practicing reflective strategies to help you assess your progress toward those goals will help set the context for your role as a lifelong learner. You may want to develop an ongoing system to make it easier for reflection to become a routine part of your day, for example, carrying around a clipboard where you can jot notes, keeping a small notebook in your desk, deciding on a specific time each day to sit and think. You'll need to develop the ways that work best for you to reflect on your own practice.

New teachers surveyed have said that they felt that they didn't change their style or approaches during their first year because no one wanted to talk about teaching and learning; they were left to rely on only themselves for thinking about their teaching (Busher, Clarke, & Taggart, 1988). Some schools now are actively encouraging collegial discussion and shared reflection on teaching practice; however, in an environment where conversation about teaching isn't encouraged, you'll need to rely on your own capacity for self-reflection in order to grow professionally and teach effectively. No matter what kind of school you're working in, however, reflection is important in helping you to constantly grow and improve as a teacher.

Reflection is more than just thinking about your day. Reflective practice involves considering questions about practice and experience in a systematic manner. If something in your class is working well, you want to understand why it is working. Conversely, if something is not working, you want to understand why not.

Reflection can be accomplished in formalized, structured ways, or by less formal, more individualized methods. Teachers can reflect in groups, sharing ideas and understandings, supporting and providing feedback for each other (Evans, 1991). Colleagues can be very helpful in examining what you're doing. Talking to others can help you to expand and grow from your experience. Reflection can occur in private, using journals or reading literature about teaching (Tama & Peterson, 1991). Sometimes reflection occurs soon after an incident;

sometimes much later. There are many first person accounts of teaching in which the writer reflects on experiences of an earlier point in her career. These reflections inform the future practices of the writer, as well as of those of other educators. Reading this literature may help you, as a new teacher, sort through your own experiences. Several of these books are included in the resources section at the end of this chapter. The rest of this chapter examines four structured methods of reflection: journals, portfolios, classroom inquiry, and feedback from others.

JOURNALS

The act of writing encourages thinking and can facilitate learning. Journal writing is an active process that can help you make explicit and connect your thoughts and experiences, analyzing them and synthesizing or combining them so that you can make meaning out of your experiences (Emig, 1977).

Writing gives you time to think about your experiences and to go back and reread what you've written. The act of writing, rereading, and writing again enables you to process your thoughts. Journal writing is personal; you choose to write about what is important to you at your own pace. It allows you to record your thoughts and to look back later and analyze your development. Writing allows you to remember your experiences over time. It's a structured way of making sense of what you've been doing.

Journal writing requires some discipline. You must be diligent and consistent, although writing every day isn't necessary. If you decide to keep a journal, contract with yourself the number of times a week you will make entries and allow time to ponder. Use the journal to record your experiences and write your impressions, questions, and feelings as well. Use the time to try to figure out some of the puzzling situations you've recently encountered. Try to do some problem-solving during this uninterrupted time. Journal writing is an opportunity to let off steam too.

If you're required to keep a journal during student teaching, there may be a specific format that you must use, or your instructor may let you use whatever format is best for you. Some people write fairly complete accounts of everything that occurred on a particular day or during a specific time period, along with their thoughts about, and analysis of aspects of the day. Others find it more practical and useful to record the high and low points of the day, as well as any insights they may have had as a result of reflection. Some people write long, involved journal entries; others write short bullets. If you have a choice, you'll need to decide what makes sense for you. In this book, we've been giving you exercises which we suggest you write in your journal. These exercises will help you focus your reflections and problem-solving on specific topics which will help you to understand your school and your experiences.

You're probably familiar with various types of journals from your teacher preparation program. You undoubtedly had to keep journals for some of your classes and learned to use them with children. For example:

- ❏ Personal journals are like diaries where you record your personal thoughts or recount events in your day.
- ❏ A dialogue journal is essentially a conversation in writing, where two people write and respond to each other.
- ❏ Literary response journals involve reacting in writing to something that you have read (Yellin & Blake, 1994).

For the purpose of promoting your own reflection during the hectic beginning year of teaching, you should choose the type of journal which best meets your needs and is still realistically doable. If you have a teaching buddy or a mentor or are a student teacher with a supervisor, a dialogue response journal might be appropriate, for example. If you are doing a lot of reading about teaching, you may want to incorporate aspects of a literary response journal. Remember that your journal needs to be personally meaningful to you in helping you to make sense of your teaching experience. You can use what you've learned about journals to help you think about what kind of journal you'd like to keep.

PORTFOLIOS

As a beginning point in the process of reflection, it's useful to set professional goals. Just as setting goals and objectives for students helps us to see changes and progress in them, setting goals for ourselves helps us to think about what we have done and to assess our own progress. Just as goal-setting for our students helps us to determine future directions for teaching, professional goal-setting helps us to ascertain our own future directions. Without setting realistic, observable goals, we may become discouraged and may not be aware of our own accomplishments. We also might miss opportunities for growth, for seeing the areas which still need work. Some examples of goals might be the following:

- ❑ I will be able to adapt lessons to various skill levels of students.
- ❑ I will develop a plan for working with parents.
- ❑ I will implement the components of the plan for working with parents.
- ❑ I will develop an integrated curriculum unit, teach it, critique it, and revise it.

If at all possible, you'll want not only to set goals, but also to document growth toward achieving these goals. One way to do this is to begin a teacher portfolio. Campbell et al. (1997) describe a portfolio as "an organized, goal-driven documentation of your professional growth and achieved competence in the complex act called teaching" (p.3). Portfolios are increasingly being used as an alternative way of assessing children. They can be equally beneficial as a way of assessing professional growth of adults.

The use of portfolios for reflection has several functions. For student teachers, they allow the opportunity to reflect on course assignments; for both student and beginning teachers, they facilitate the rethinking of problematic lessons and the holistic examination of one's experience (Guillaume & Yopp, 1995). If you're able to keep a portfolio during the course of your teaching career, saving evidence related to your teaching and other professional activities and responsibilities will help you to see changes in your teaching over time. This kind of documentation can be especially helpful if you find yourself, as most teachers do, repeating lessons or units. You'll actually be able to systematically analyze ways in which you've changed your lessons and think about how and why you've made changes, as well as whether you've improved the lessons.

Many states now require that teachers be periodically recertified. In order to provide evidence of professional development activities for recertification, teachers may need to develop a professional development plan and document progress towards the goals stated in the plan. A portfolio is an effective way of collecting and exhibiting evidence. Merely keeping a file of conference programs, certificates of attendance, and lesson plans is not sufficient to warrant calling this collection of evidence a portfolio. Reflection on the activities and an organizational structure which relates the various activities to stated professional goals are also necessary. You must select materials which are meaningful to you, and also clearly relevant to your goals.

As a student teacher, the development of a portfolio can be useful in demonstrating professional growth for a college supervisor and ultimately for a prospective employer. Many colleges now require that students in education programs develop a portfolio during their teacher preparation program. Various types of materials may be included in your portfolio in order to give a picture of who you are and to provide evidence of your competence and growth as a professional in different arenas. Some of the areas that may be represented include:

- ❏ evidence of personal traits, interests, and general qualifications
- ❏ evidence of your ability to develop curricula
- ❏ evidence, through student work, of students' responses to your work
- ❏ evidence of your involvement with parents and the community
- ❏ evidence of your research on or inquiry into particular issues and your reflection upon them
- ❏ evidence of your ability to work with a range of students with varied backgrounds and learning needs
- ❏ evidence of your ability to collaborate and coordinate well with other faculty

In order to demonstrate these abilities you might include items such as lesson plans and units, samples of student work, correspondence with parents, materials you've designed, presentations or papers you've written (Mary McMackin, n.d.).

Portfolios are not necessarily a reflection only of one's best work. You should include samples of lessons that may not have been successful, along with your thinking about why this may have happened. Remember that the function of one type of portfolio is to show growth. In other portfolios, those for employers, for example, you may want to showcase your best work. As a tool to aid in reflection, however, including examples of less successful endeavors can ultimately make you a better teacher. Think of the benefits of looking back at your portfolio and tracing your professional growth and learning. The combination of inquiry into why a lesson or approach may or may not have worked (explained later in this chapter) and inclusion in a portfolio can be very powerful. Portfolios kept by your students can also aid in your own reflection. Not only do you see their progress in learning, but you also see your progress in teaching. Examining your students' growth will help you to assess your own effectiveness.

Many of these ideas would be useful for a teacher portfolio as well as for a student teacher portfolio. Remember that materials collected must relate to goals, and that a reflection and rationale are important components of the portfolio. If you continue to work on your portfolio over time, looking through it, removing and adding things as you deem appropriate, this will be a very helpful way for you to assess and reflect on your professional growth and your teaching practice. Although this process may sound like a burden, you should remember that it is your work, and you decide on what will be personally meaningful. If you are documenting for an outside source, such as a certification agency, you will need to reflect on the goals which are required.

> ### 7.1 Exercise for Your Journal:
> ### Beginning a Portfolio
>
> Formulate one goal for your teaching during the next month. List several pieces of evidence you could collect which might help you to demonstrate your progress toward this goal.

CLASSROOM INQUIRY / TEACHER RESEARCH

Still another important tool for reflection is classroom-based inquiry, action research, or teacher research. This type of inquiry or research involves thinking about an issue or practice in your teaching, finding a way to state it as a question about which you can collect data, and collecting the relevant information. You can think about this inquiry as the pursuit of "wonderings" about your teaching through the formulation and reformulation of questions and descriptions of data collected to attempt to answer these questions (Hubbard & Power, 1993).

Reflective teachers are constantly asking questions about their teaching. Teacher researchers pay more careful attention to what's happening in their classrooms. Simply stated, the process of inquiry helps you figure out what is working and what is not. Some examples of inquiry questions might be the following:

- ❑ Do I call on boys and girls equally during math?
- ❑ Do author's studies affect the number of books my students choose to read?
- ❑ Does the use of manipulatives affect Susan's ability to solve math problems?
- ❑ Will the implementation of a social skills curriculum increase students' positive behaviors towards each other?
- ❑ What is the effect on behavior in the cafeteria of the discipline program instituted at my school?

Although it may sound as though beginning teachers would have difficulty engaging in action research, it can be very important in helping teachers to develop habits of reflective practice (Tickle,1994). At many colleges, an inquiry component is an integral part of the preparation of teachers. When you learn to do action research early in your career, you're more likely to develop a lifelong habit of systematically formulating questions and collecting data to help you reflect on and inform your practice. Once life begins to settle down for you in your school, you can use this process to supplement the often intuitive, anecdotal approach to understanding practice that has traditionally been characteristic of schools and teachers. We're not recommending that you ignore your intuition, only that you also engage in more systematic data collection as well. Your intuitive hunches might well be the starting point, the motivation, for the development of your questions. Inquiry will make your job easier, not harder. The goal of inquiry is to help you understand how to teach more effectively.

Some colleges and schools, especially Professional Development Schools, are increasingly offering support groups and courses for people interested in pursuing action research. If you work in such a school, try to take advantage of the opportunities offered. Initially, it would be especially valuable for you to join a group rather than attempting to engage in such research on your own. The support and feedback of "critical friends," whose role it is to ask "leading questions that enabled the teacher to clarify her thinking and make decisions about the action she would take" (Hopkins, 1993, p.18) will help you along in the process. In schools where there is a culture of collaboration and where co-teaching or team teaching are being practiced, teachers can observe one another to help in collecting data. In addition, an inquiry group can be a network which helps to reduce some of the isolation and stress associated with teaching. The work of the group must be well integrated into the daily work of teaching, so that it doesn't feel as though it's adding to the stress of the job.

"Undertaking research in their own and colleagues' classrooms is one way in which teachers can take increased responsibility for their actions and create a more energetic and dynamic environment in which teaching and learning can occur" (Hopkins, 1993, p.1). Don't underestimate the value of such inquiry. If you've begun doing it in your teacher preparation program, keep it up. The practice of classroom-based action research can actually help to transform the culture of a school; as a new teacher, engaging in such research may be one way to act as a change agent. The effect goes beyond the individual classroom. As teachers work together, ideas generated can influence the school as a whole. An in-depth discussion of classroom inquiry is beyond the scope of this book. Readings on this topic are provided in the resources section at the end of this chapter, and we would recommend that you turn to these for more information.

> ### 7.2 Exercise for Your Journal:
> ### Formulating a Research Question
>
> Think about a question you have about your teaching, or an area which you would like to improve. Brainstorm and write in your journal ways you might state this as a question about which you could collect observable data. Think about and note what types of data you might be able to collect in order to begin to answer your question. If you are in a seminar and you have an opportunity, discuss questions with others in your group.

FEEDBACK FROM OTHERS

Another way to facilitate reflection in teaching is to ask others to give you feedback and to engage in discussion with them about your practice. Children in your class, parents, and other teachers, all may provide useful information which will help you evaluate your teaching. For example, colleagues can be helpful not only in inquiry groups and in other types of networking or support groups, discussed elsewhere in this chapter, but also in peer coaching activities. Peer coaching is explored more fully in Chapter Six, but essentially it involves structured, collegial observation and feedback on one's teaching over a period of time. Clearly, the opportunity to learn new ways to teach, to observe and be observed by others, to receive feedback, and to engage in discussions over time is an invaluable tool for reflection. In this section of the chapter, we'll explore several different ways in which teachers can use feedback from others to help them reflect on their teaching.

The Rounds Model

Traditionally, American teachers have had very few, if any, opportunities to observe other teachers teach. In other countries, such as Japan and China, as part of their induction year, new teachers watch other teachers, discuss practice, critique and present demonstration lessons, and discuss and simulate with colleagues the responses of students to various presentations of material (Darling-Hammond, 1998). In the U.S., we rarely provide student, beginning, or veteran teachers such opportunities for collegial exchange and reflection about a shared observation of teaching practice. Yet think of the value of such experiences! Linda Darling-Hammond quotes one high school teacher, a twenty-five year veteran, as saying, "I have taught 20,000 classes, I have been evaluated 30 times, but I have never seen another teacher teach" (1998, p.10).

Clearly, new models for meaningful collegial interchange must be developed. The "Rounds" or "Grand Rounds" process, borrowed from the medical profession, is one approach to creating such opportunities for shared reflection on practice using a common experience of observing teaching in action. This model is most commonly implemented in Professional Development Schools, where there is a commitment from a college and school to sharing practice. However, it could be done in any school with a commitment to collaboration and reflection.

The Rounds Model generally involves a group of preservice and/or inservice teachers meeting together with an education faculty member and/ or school administrator for a brief (15-20 minute) pre-conference to discuss objectives, issues, and strategies of classroom practice which they will subsequently observe in action (Flagg St.-Assumption College PDS brochure, n.d.). Structuring of the process varies, but generally the observations are guided by prepared questions (DelPrete, 1997). Next, the group observes the teaching of lessons in a teacher's classroom. The final component of the model involves a post-observation conference where the classroom teacher debriefs with the group, focussing on understanding and reflecting on what happened during the observation.

The "Rounds" model is one way of building shared reflection and collaborative inquiry into the process of teaching. Implementing rounds or another similar structure can both enhance the collegiality of teachers, whether they be new, experienced, or student teachers, and create a community of learners within a school. If you have the opportunity to work in a school where this kind of activity is done and encouraged, you should seriously consider getting involved. Your ability to reflect on your practice will be greatly enhanced.

Feedback from Teachers

Asking for feedback from your colleagues, although it may feel threatening at first, can be a most rewarding and instructive experience. Although this works best when there is a peer coaching model or a Rounds Model, with a framework developed for giving feedback, you should make an effort to create opportunities for observing and being observed even if there is no structured program in your school. When engaging in these kinds of reflective discussions with peers, it is important that the tone and manner with which feedback is given is a collegial, friendly one and does not sound condescending or evaluative. As you think about choosing colleagues to give you such feedback, consider all that you know about your school and your peers. You may be part of a team that will naturally work together to give each other mutual feedback. In any case, choose someone whom you trust, who is discreet, and whose teaching skills and subject matter knowledge you respect.

7.3 Exercise for Your Journal:
   Getting Feedback from Teachers

The following questions may help guide you in asking for feedback from your peers. Some questions may be more appropriate when feedback is requested on one lesson in particular, and others may be better suited to feedback given in association with observations done over a period of time. The questions listed here are only examples. Specific questions or areas for attention must be tailored to your circumstances to be most helpful.

This type of feedback could lend itself well to a classroom inquiry question. In fact, rather than ask a colleague to comment on too many aspects of teaching behavior, it might be better to focus on a specific area or question on which you would like to collect data and direct his observations to that question.

Choose a question or set of questions which reflect an area of your teaching on which you would like feedback. Ask a colleague to come into your class and observe you, focussing attention on the question(s) which you have chosen. Set up a time before the observation to discuss what you would like the focus to be and how data might be collected and a time after the observation to debrief and discuss what she observed. Record in your journal the questions, highlights of the discussion, and your own reflections based on what you learned. Think about how it felt to engage in this process, how you reacted to hearing the feedback, i.e., whether it seemed to make sense to you, how what you learned might impact your work, follow-up observations, and other next steps.

- Were my directions clear?
- Were the purposes of the lesson clear?
- Were the children engaged? How did you know? What evidence was there of this engagement or non-engagement?
- Please comment on:
  - my interactions with children
  - tone of voice
  - smiling
  - sarcasm
  - humor
  - classroom management techniques
- Did I call on girls and boys equally? (You might actually have your observer count behaviors, for example, the number of times you call on boys and girls.)
- Please comment on questioning techniques, as well as my response to questions from children.
- Did I call on children all around the room or was I concentrating on certain areas of the classroom?
- Was I in command of the subject matter? Did I seem to know the material?
- Can you describe movement in the classroom, of both teacher and children?

Feedback from Parents

It can be extremely helpful to ask for feedback from parents. You will get a perspective on how information is communicated to the home and how the children in your class are talking about what goes on in school. You probably want to send home a questionnaire two or three times a year. More often than that might be overwhelming to parents and less often would not give you enough information to affect your teaching practices.

Some parents may welcome the opportunity to give you feedback. The questionnaire itself will make them feel more involved in their child's education and in itself will serve as a means of communication and home-school connection. You might consider asking parents how frequently they would like to complete these questionnaires. For other ideas about communicating with families, look at Chapter Four.

7.4 Exercise for Your Journal: Getting Feedback from Parents

Questions such as the following will give you helpful information from parents. You should develop your own questions for specific purposes. Within the first two months of school, send home with your students a questionnaire, based on the following questions. Omit or add questions so that the feedback will best meet your needs. In your journal, write an analysis of the responses you received. Reflect on the implications of the responses for your teaching. Think about how you felt receiving this information, how you will incorporate the response you received into your teaching practice, what will be your next steps.

- Was communication between school and home helpful and clear?
- How does your child describe her school day?
- What kinds of things has your child been saying about what we've been doing this month?
- Would you have liked more opportunities for involvement in your child's school life? What kinds of involvement?
- Do you feel that your child has been happy this year?
- Has she mentioned any issues of concern? Explain.

- Do you have any concerns? Explain.
- Please comment on the homework. Is there too much? Too little? Too difficult? Too easy?
- How did you feel about your involvement in your child's homework? Was it too much? Too little?

Feedback from Children

Still another avenue for feedback is the children in your class. You can learn a great deal from talking to your students about their perceptions. There are many ways to do this, and, of course, all must be done carefully. You certainly don't want to let loose a barrage of criticism which would be damaging to your self-esteem and which would empower your children inappropriately. However, depending on the age level and maturity of your class, you may find various devices for engaging them in a constructive conversation. Pollard & Tann (1987) suggest several ideas for such activity. For example, they suggest having a discussion, with the class or with small groups, about what makes a good teacher, having children write about their ideal school, asking children to write reports or report cards on your performance during the year, perhaps at the time when you are doing so for them.

Freiberg (1995, chap. 3) has developed a Teacher Effectiveness Questionnaire, which provides for student feedback and is used from the fourth grade through the twelfth grade. He recommends using this questionnaire in conjunction with a self-assessment measure, which provides data on six areas of student-teacher interaction: questioning, teacher/student talk, opening and closing of the lesson, wait-time, praise statements, and use of student ideas. The classroom is tape-recorded for 20-45 minutes, and then the tape is analyzed according to the areas on the instrument.

At the college level, students are generally asked to evaluate courses and instructors, yet we rarely ask K-12 students to do the same. In an informal survey of children in middle and high school, only one or two had ever been asked to evaluate a teacher, and those had only participated in evaluation once or twice during their careers in school. Yet, when asked about teachers, they had had, they were interested in discussing what made teachers "good" or "bad" and had wise and logical advice to give new teachers. For student teachers who are accustomed to doing such course evaluations in their own education, this type of student evaluation could be especially useful. Clearly, if you collect such information from children, you must use it wisely to aid in reflection. You must analyze patterns and think about reasons for certain types of comments. You must translate comments into suggestions for teaching which make sense, given the context of your class, school, and your personality. You need to think about the implications of children's perspectives for your teaching. Listen to your students and try not to get defensive. They are the ultimate consumers of your service, and they are the ones who must benefit from your work. Their ideas may be simple and doable and may give you valuable insight into your professional effectiveness.

7.5 Exercise for Your Journal:
Getting Feedback from Children

Too often we forget (or are afraid) to ask the very people who are most directly affected by our teaching — our students. Students can give us a valuable perspective on our teaching in general and on specific aspects of what we do. It will be most helpful to ask these questions periodically, so that you can get ongoing feedback. The following questions may help you to get the kind of information you need to reflect on and improve your practice. These questions are intended to provide a beginning framework. Feel free to adapt or add questions to make this exercise appropriate to your specific situation and needs. The wording of questions will need to be adapted to various grade levels. For young children, the questions will need not only to be simplified, but also to be administered orally. During the first month of school, give two questionnaires to your students. On one questionnaire, you should ask them questions, such as those in the first part of this exercise, which relate to specifics of a lesson that you have taught and the activities you have been doing in class. On the second questionnaire, you can ask more general questions to solicit their opinions about teachers in general. In your journal, analyze their responses to the questionnaires, write about and reflect on your reactions, reflect on the implications of their responses for your teaching practice, i.e., how will this affect what you do, and what are your next steps?

- What did you like most about the lesson (unit, project, activity)?
- What did you like least?
- If I were to teach this again, what should I do differently?
- What would make it more fun? More interesting?
- What should I keep the same?
- What is one thing you learned from this?
- What do you think about the activities we've been doing for the past month?
- Have they been fun?
- What are the three most interesting things you've learned?

You can also ask children more general questions about teaching. Some general questions you might ask are:

- What do you think makes a good teacher?
- What are your least favorite things about a teacher?
- What do some teachers do that you do/don't like?
- What advice would you give to new teachers?

Of course, in order to get honest responses from children, you must develop a classroom climate of trust and respect. If children are afraid to say anything critical, you will most likely not get honest feedback from them. Think about how you can develop a classroom culture where people talk and work together to create the best possible environment for learning.

7.6 Exercise for Your Journal: Thinking About Ways to Get Feedback

Brainstorm (alone or with a partner) all the ways that you could, throughout the year, help children feel safe in talking about teaching and learning. Think about activities, ways of talking with children about their own learning and about yours, ways that you give feedback to children.

Feedback from Supervisors

Another avenue for self reflection can come from the evaluation done by supervisors. School systems generally have a formal evaluation process, especially for teachers in their first year, but also for experienced teachers. Make sure that you find out about your school's evaluation process. Student teachers, of course, are evaluated in order to determine teaching competence; this evaluation is usually done by the college supervisor and the cooperating teacher/mentor with whom the student works. Although some of these evaluations, especially those of experienced teachers may seem perfunctory, you can make an effort to use the feedback to help you reflect on your teaching.

Hopefully, you will be able to engage your evaluator(s) in meaningful discussion of their observations. You may be able to have a pre-conference where you request that you be observed in areas where you would like help and where you are able to set goals for the evaluation. If you participate in a conference after the observation, you may be asked to evaluate yourself before the supervisor gives you feedback. Use these opportunities to analyze your practice. Although you may feel anxious about being observed and evaluated, try to think of the experience as a way to become a better teacher. Take control of the discussion as much as possible, by anticipating problematic issues and thinking about solutions. Don't hesitate to point out your strengths either. It's probably more important to understand why your teaching is successful than why something may not work. In any case, you should be able to articulate your hypotheses for either success or failure.

If you are fortunate as a new teacher, you may have a mentor who actually observes you and gives you feedback without evaluating you. This relationship can be a very useful aid in reflection. Mentoring is discussed in greater detail in Chapter Six. As you read that chapter, think about ways that a mentor can help you become a more reflective practitioner.

Informal Conversations with Colleagues

Another way to reflect on your teaching is to engage in problem-solving with others through informal conversations in the Teachers' Room, after school, or anywhere you find yourself with the opportunity to talk. This kind of informal collaboration can result in the sharing of useful information, the exchange of ideas and tips about teaching, the analysis of one's teaching practice, and joint problem-solving. This type of conversation not only helps improve individual teaching and student learning, but it also increases the effectiveness of the whole school. Unfortunately, many schools do not have a culture which supports such interactions. The talk in many Teachers' Rooms centers on complaints about work, children, and families or on shopping and sports. "Instead of mere grousing, faculty interaction in effective schools centers on the work of teachers and ways to improve it . . . professional dialogue in effective schools centers not so much on people as on problems" (Rosenholtz & Kyle, 1984).

As we have discussed throughout this book, the culture of many schools in which isolation is the norm promotes the view that if you discuss problems or ask for advice, you are admitting incompetence. Conversely, if you offer advice or suggestions, you are assuming superiority (Rosenholtz & Kyle, 1984). In schools where the culture promotes isolation, you'll need to turn to more self-directed means of reflection, or to find one or two trusted colleagues with whom you can speak freely. You can also seek out contact with other teachers from outside your school or school system. If you are fortunate enough to find yourself in a school where there is a culture of collaboration, you may find frequent opportunities with colleagues for analysis of and reflection on your own teaching. As a new teacher, take some time to discern the norms of your school. Refer back to earlier chapters for tools which will help you do this.

SUMMARY

In this chapter, we've discussed several techniques to help you reflect on your teaching. Some are structured and formalized; some are informal. At times you'll reflect by yourself, using individualized tools like journals and sometimes you'll get input from and share your thoughts with others to help you make sense of and refine your practice. What's important is that you find the ways that feel right to you, and you take the time to do it. Try as often as possible to go over what has happened in your day and to analyze your successes and challenges. Reflection will not only make you a better teacher, but it will also help you to be energized and to find satisfaction in your chosen profession.

Suggested Resources

Ashton-Warner, S. (1963). *Teacher*. New York: Simon and Schuster.

Campbell, D.M., Cignetti, P.B., Melenyzer, B.J., Nettles. D.H., &Wyman, R.M. Jr. (1997). *How to develop a professional portfolio: A manual for teachers*. Needham Heights, MA: Allyn and Bacon.

Costantino, P.M. & De Lorenzo, M.N. (2002). *Developing a professional teaching portfolio: A guide for success*. Boston: Allyn and Bacon.

Hubbard, R.S. & Power, B.M. (1993). *The art of classroom inquiry*. Portsmouth, N.H.: Heinemann.

Hubbard, R.S. & Power, B.M. (1999). *Living the questions: A guide for teacher-researchers*. York, ME: Stenhouse.

Kane, P.R. (1991). *The first year of teaching: Real world stories from America's teachers*. New York: Mentor.

Kidder, T. (1989). *Among schoolchildren*. Boston: Houghton Mifflin.

Palmer, P.J. (1998). *The courage to teach*. San Francisco: Jossey-Bass.

Schubert, W.H. & Ayers, W.A., Eds. (1992). *Teacher lore: Learning from our own experience*. White Plains, NY: Longman.

CHAPTER EIGHT

THE BURNOUT PROBLEM: HOW TO AVOID IT

Burnout is a syndrome of emotional exhaustion, deperson-alization, and reduced personal accomplishment that can occur among individuals who do 'people work' of some kind. It is a response to the chronic emotional strain of dealing extensively with other human beings, particularly when they are troubled or having problems. . . . what is unique about burnout is that the stress arises from the social inter-action between helper and recipient. (Maslach, 1982, p.3)

During student teaching and in your beginning teaching years, you can expect to feel tired and perhaps even stressed! There is so much to do, and time always seems to be at a premium. You are in a profession where you can feel as though you are giving of yourself and "on stage" all day long. In teaching, there is always more to do than seems possi-ble for one person. Another source of frustration is the perceived gap between the new teacher's ideals and goals and the realities of the ordinary routines of teaching. If you feel unsupported or isolated, as beginning teachers often do, feeling stressed or burned out is a poten-tial danger; you should be aware of the signs and of possible solutions. The isolation and frustration felt by teachers seems to result in teach-ers leaving the profession early in their careers. Two-thirds to three-quarters of teachers who leave the field do so during their first four years (Rosenholtz & Kyle, 1984).

In order to cope with the many demands, it's essential to learn to prioritize and to be satisfied with accomplishing a few things well. It is important to continue to maintain a positive outlook on your accom-plishments and to remember why you are in this profession. Although you are giving much of yourself, you are also receiving so much. If you are not careful, it is easy to get into a complaining mode of behavior.

Learn to see the humor in everyday activities and allow yourself to feel joy! Seek out the company of people who will laugh with you. Being around children has enormous potential for bringing humor into your lives. Allow them to laugh, and allow yourself to delight in their laughter. To be sure, education is serious business, but it should be fun too!

The reality though is that you may feel conflicted about the day to day, minute to minute demands on you and the desire and responsibility you feel to make your classroom an exciting place for your children and your job a source of professional growth and excitement. There is a level of routine in teaching, certain regularities in the structure of each day, in working with the same children (Sarason, 1996). This routinization may differ from the ideals and expectations new teachers bring from their training. Unfortunately, this gap alienates some new teachers from teaching and may contribute to their leaving the profession during the first years.

This chapter addresses some danger signs of burnout and discusses strategies for its prevention and cure. Even if you don't feel these symptoms yourself, you may see colleagues who do exhibit such signs. After reading this chapter, you will be better able to understand their experience and feelings and may be able to provide them support. In this chapter and in other parts of this book, we suggest proactive approaches to sustaining yourself and promoting professional satisfaction during your early teaching years and later on in your career; we include suggestions for taking care of yourself, as well as finding professional communities and networks for support and professional growth.

CAUSES AND SYMPTOMS OF STRESS AND BURNOUT

There are many reasons why teachers may experience stress. The demands of teaching are many and varied. As we've discussed, teachers are expected to play many roles and to meet many different expectations. As a new teacher, the demands of these expectations are further complicated and exacerbated by the new responsibilities you may be facing as you move out of the world of the student and into the professional realm. Moving into the adult role or changing professions, you may find yourself juggling different personal as well as professional responsibilities. In this section, we will look at some of the causes and symptoms of stress and burnout.

The Demands of Teaching

Student teachers and new teachers may feel overwhelmed by the many dimensions of teaching and the need to be skilled in managing groups, facilitating positive behavior, planning motivating activities, collecting needed resources and responding to the individual needs of a large group of students. Furthermore, as a student teacher you are often struggling to figure out your own teaching style. Even though you are a novice in the profession, the demands of teaching seemingly require you to master the multifaceted aspects of the profession right from the beginning. You may be spending many hours planning lessons and preparing for each day. Phillip W. Jackson, in his classic study, *Life in Classrooms*, (1968) suggests that elementary teachers engage in personal interactions each day which require up to a thousand decisions. Some of these are the result of study and planning, but because of the nature of classrooms, many are instantaneous. Like any new complex activity, for a person without an experience base, this kind of on-your-feet decision making can be exhausting and draining of emotional energy.

If you are a student teacher, additional stress may be caused by teaching in someone else's classroom, constantly trying to understand their perspectives on teaching and their classroom practice. The reality of the day to day demands of the profession may come as a surprise. Many student teachers are also taking additional courses at the college or university or working part-time and feel stretched in many different directions. All of these factors can lead to stress.

Juggling New Roles

A major source of stress for many new teachers is the difficulty inherent in beginning two new roles in life: that of the professional teacher and the emerging adult. For many of you, not only is this your first time employed as a teacher, with the awesome responsibility for the lives of children, but this is also your first time living away from home or a college dorm, with all of the responsibilities involved in maintaining your own apartment and your independent life. You may have moved to a community where you don't know anyone or have embarked on a new marriage. What an overwhelming combination of new life experiences! You may be feeling that coping with any one of these changes would be more than you can effectively handle.

For those of you who are beginning teaching with families of your own, the stresses are certainly no less intense. An increasing number of teachers are parents themselves, as more people choose teaching as their second or third career, and more women continue to work after they have families. How do you tend to the needs of your own children, your class, your spouse or partner, and yourself? How do you help your own children with homework, while doing your own 'home work'? Balancing work and home, each with its own set of intense interpersonal demands, and still finding time for yourself, is a difficult challenge.

Symptoms of Burnout

Many helping professions assist novices in recognizing and learning some strategies for dealing with stress and for addressing the signs of burnout. An excellent description of teacher burnout can be found in the book *Professional Burnout in Human Service Organizations* (Cherniss, 1980). The key features of burnout, according to Cherniss, are negative changes in attitudes and behaviors relating to work including a growing pessimism about one's work, decline in motivation, and a tendency to distance oneself from and to feel anger towards clients and colleagues. Other symptoms include being preoccupied with one's own comfort and welfare on the job; rationalizing failure by blaming the clients or 'the system'; and being resistant to change, becoming increasingly rigid, and losing creativity.

One must also be aware of possible physical and psychological changes which may be indicators of burnout, such as "chronic fatigue; frequent colds; the flu, headaches, gastrointestinal disturbances, and sleeplessness; excessive use of drugs; decline in self-esteem; and marital and family conflict"(Cherniss, pp.6-7).

Of course, some of these physical symptoms may be related to occupational hazards of the teaching profession. Teachers often seem to catch whatever illnesses are currently prevalent among the children in the school. Recurrent illness itself increases one's stress level. Teachers generally feel a responsibility to the children and come to work even when they feel quite ill. It's not easy to function optimally under such circumstances.

It is important, however, to be attuned to the messages coming from your body which may indicate how you are feeling about your work. If you notice many of the behavioral and physical signs listed here, it may be time to pause and consider what might really be going on, how you are feeling about what you are doing. Observing these behaviors and understanding them in yourself are an important first step. Developing varied strategies for dealing with stress and interpersonal burnout can be an important tool for long-term satisfaction in the profession.

PREVENTING STRESS AND FINDING FULFILLMENT

As a new teacher or a student teacher, it's important that you find ways to take care of yourself so you can prevent the feelings of stress that may arise and eventually lead to burnout. There are many ways to do this, some of which involve finding ways to care for and nourish yourself, and some of which involve gaining support from others. In this chapter, we will primarily explore strategies which relate to caring for yourself. In the next chapter, we'll look more carefully at ways to find support from others. You are not alone if you are feeling that you must actively think of ways to prevent or reduce stress and find fulfillment in your chosen profession.

Taking Care of Yourself

In the words of one teacher,

> Sometimes I think I can't do it all. I don't want to be bitter or a martyr so I am careful to take care of myself. I put flowers on my desk to offset the dreariness of the old school building. I leave school several times a week to run errands or to take walks in order to feel less trapped. Other teachers take courses at local colleges, join committees of adults, talk in the teachers' lounge, or play with computers. In order to give to others, teachers must nurture themselves. (Metzger & Fox, 1986)

It may sound like a cliche to say that you need to remember to take care of yourself, but it's critical that you do so. You need to determine what will help you to feel cared for and make a special effort to keep those things in your life. You need to remember, for example, to eat a nutritionally sound diet. Taking the time to think about what you eat, and preparing meals for yourself, can be nourishing for the spirit, as well as the body. Sitting down with a cup of tea can have a calming effect at the end of a long day. You may even want to treat yourself to a luxurious bubble bath.

Making time for exercise is also important. A walk at the end of the day, or at any other time that is possible, can do wonders for your psyche and your physical well-being. Seek out whatever is beautiful to you and go out of your way to see that beauty, whether it involves walking through your favorite park, strolling along the beach, or running into an art gallery. If you are a person who likes to shop, you may want to duck into a store on your way home and treat yourself to a purchase. You may feel as though you only do things for others. Buying yourself a gift can be something that you do only for yourself. Don't underestimate the value of giving yourself a treat. You can be kinder to others, with less resentment, if you can be kind to yourself as well.

When we asked experienced teachers what kinds of strategies they use and would recommend for reducing feelings of stress and/or burnout, the following were some of their suggestions:

- ◆ "I jog 5-6 miles, first thing in the morning, every day."

- ◆ "Within the school I find someone who will listen. You need to look for someone who shares your values — someone who sees children as you see them."

- ◆ "If children feel successful, then students will be more cooperative and you will have less stress. Help children feel successful every day."

- ◆ "Make sure you are well-organized."

- ◆ "Don't take a lot of work home. Plan ahead and do most of your work at school."

- ◆ "Do something very different in the summer."

- ◆ "Have a rich life after school."

- ◆ "Exercise daily."

- ◆ "Make sure you take one day for yourself on weekends."

- ◆ "Eat lunch and socialize."

- ◆ "Listen to music."

Some of the other ways in which you can take care of yourself include limiting your commitments, getting away from work, managing your time, finding professional satisfaction, and developing coping skills. These strategies are described in more detail in the following sections.

Limiting your commitments

One way to combat the development and growth of some of these symptoms may be to reduce or eliminate involvement in outside commitments, both related and unrelated to school. One of the new teachers whom we interviewed said that the most memorable and useful advice given by the superintendent during the district orientation was to say no to participation in committees, regardless of what people say you should do. This teacher was able to use this advice when asked by her principal to join particular committees. Her decision was respected, and she felt that she was better able to devote her energies to teaching. Several new teachers in our beginning teachers support group echoed these sentiments by saying that the best advice they could give to new teachers was to set a few goals and to not try to do too much or make too many changes during the first year. There will be many future opportunities for such involvement; the delay of a year or two is wise.

You may not want to refuse to participate in committees, however. If you believe that, because of the culture of the school or the expectations of the principal, lack of participation will result in ostracism or negative evaluations of your performance, you'll need to take that into consideration in making your decisions. Getting involved in one committee may be important in order to help you meet people and find allies in the school. You also want to project an image of a responsible colleague who meets her obligations. Think, however, about whether you might be able to postpone joining for a year, while you get your feet on the ground. Even if the opportunities that present themselves are very appealing, be cautious about getting involved in too many activities. You may find yourself having difficulty doing any of them well. Remember that your first priority is to find support for yourself as a beginning teacher, so that you can be successful with the children whom you teach.

Getting away from your work

It is critical, at every stage of life, to find ways to nourish yourself and to get away entirely from your work. Teaching is intense work, and vacations are times to rejuvenate yourself so that you can continue to give to your students, parents and colleagues. A total change of pace during vacation and getting away or engaging in activities that are unrelated to your work, but that refresh you as a human being, are critically important. You may find as a student teacher or as a new teacher that you are thinking about your job twenty-four hours a day. You may have a key to the school and may be staying past 7:00 PM and still not making a dent in what you feel needs to be accomplished. You may have to leave the building at 3:30 but are taking piles of work home and burning the midnight oil, and waking up exhausted. You may not be sleeping well and may be worrying about work when you wake up at one or two in the morning. You are probably juggling multiple demands such as courses and work or work and family. It is critically important to find ways to get away and refresh yourself whether it is through sports, socializing, a weekend or vacation away, or pursuit of interests unrelated to teaching.

Managing your time

> People who efficiently manage their time have learned to structure their lives so that they focus most of their time and energy on what is most important to them and minimize the time they spend on activities they do not value. (Davis, Eshelman, & McKay, 1995, p.167)

Vilfredo Pareto, an Italian economist, has said that 20% of what we do yields 80% of the results, and 80% of what we do yields 20% of the results (Davis, et al, 1995). You can apply this to your own life to help you set priorities. You should clarify the important ways to spend your time and focus on those. Try to maximize the amount of time you spend on activities which will produce the results which you want and need, rather than spending most of your time engaged in useless, non-productive activities. Being able to set priorities, to clarify what is really important, and to manage your time more effectively will help reduce your level of stress.

The key components or tasks of time management include: clarifying your values, setting goals, developing an action plan, evaluating how you spend your time, combatting procrastination, and organizing your time (Davis, Eshelman, & McKay, 1995). The Davis, et al workbook includes a series of exercises to assist you in each of these steps. Completion of activities or exercises which help you to think about how the ways in which you spend your time relate to your values and goals, can be beneficial to you as you begin your teaching career.

There will undoubtedly be many competitors for your time, both at your teaching job and in your life in general. You may find it useful to think about these tasks in the larger context of all of your life's roles and in the various roles you play as a teacher. It's important for you to manage all aspects of your life and to figure out how and where your work fits. It's equally important for you to determine how you will balance the many expectations and responsibilities you have as a teacher. Effective time management is critical for teachers at all levels of experience. It is especially important when, as a new teacher, you are faced with developing yourself as a professional and perhaps even as an adult. Priorities will become easier to determine the more experience you have.

If you are going to engage in activities which we have discussed elsewhere in this book, such as those which promote reflection and those which reduce stress, you'll need to consciously build these into your day. These activities will need to be part of your values, your goals, and your action plan. Some people find it helpful to set aside specific times, weekly or daily, or even to make appointments with themselves.

Finding professional satisfaction

Another way to prevent or help alleviate burnout is to find ways to rejuvenate yourself professionally. Even beginning teachers can consider various professional opportunities, as long as they are not too time-consuming or overwhelming. If you or your school have an affiliation with a college, for example, you might offer to speak to a class or student teaching seminar about the experience of a beginning teacher. People who have done this have reported it to be a very satisfying experience, which not only benefits the individual, but provides a critical perspective for the student teachers. Becoming part of a study group or book group can also be an intellectually stimulating experience which can add to your professional growth and can help in your practice. Be cautious, however, about overcommitting yourself or adding to the pressure you might already feel.

Another stimulating role might be to work with a preservice teacher. Although new teachers are generally not eligible to supervise practicum students, they may be able to work with a pre-practicum student, or to just mentor a student teacher in the building. If you are a student teacher, you might team with another student teacher to create and conduct a lesson or series of lessons in both your classes.

Working with another adult in your classroom can help to provide an opportunity for you to reflect on your own practice and sharpen your skills. It can also provide an opportunity for new learning and mutual support. As we know from cooperative group work with children, teaching others can be a very effective way to learn. The interaction between teaching and learning is an invigorating experience.

Sharing ideas with a student teacher in a mentoring role can be a very stimulating activity, since you can think out loud with another person. You may find a greater degree of like-mindedness and support for your own ideas with a preservice teacher than from veteran teachers in your building. This support in itself can help to prevent burnout by providing stimulation and contact with another adult. Be careful, however, that you do not develop alliances only with student teachers, or you might jeopardize your chances of forming important relationships with your colleagues. For more ideas on finding professional satisfaction through collegial relationships, refer to Chapter Six on working with colleagues.

Developing coping skills

Cooley and Yovanoff (1996) taught coping skills to special educators, a group at especially high risk for burnout. Teaching them specific coping skills and pairing them up to encourage supportive peer collaboration around work-related problems reduced stress and burnout and increased job satisfaction. Teachers participated in workshops focused on teaching three main types of coping skills: skills for changing the situation, which involved identifying what can be changed about a given situation and problem-solving to develop an action plan to create solutions (situational); skills for changing the physical response to a situation, such as muscle relaxation techniques (physiological); skills for changing how one thinks about a situation (cognitive), which involved recognizing distorted beliefs, as well as self or peer-coaching to change one's way of thinking.

As a student teacher or beginning teacher, you can learn strategies similar to those described here. You may wish to practice various responses to problematic and stressful situations based on these three strategies. Look at the "Coping Skills Strategies Worksheets" to help you apply these strategies to real situations in your life. The "Exercise for your Journal: Applying Coping Skills" provides vignettes that you can use to practice applying the strategies to situations that other teachers have described to us.

Coping Skills Strategies Worksheets

Worksheet for Situational Coping Skills

According to Cooley and Yovanoff (1996), the situational coping strategy involves identifying the problem situation, identifying what can be changed, and problem-solving to develop an action plan to create solutions. The following worksheet, based on their work, should create a framework which will help you to analyze the problem and begin to think about possible solutions. This might be done best with a supportive partner. Think carefully about who that might be.

I. Describe the problem situation
   • Who is involved?
   • What is the nature of the problem? Describe clearly.
   • Why is it a problem?
   • How long has the situation been going on?

II. Identification of what can and cannot be changed
   • What needs to change in order for the problem to be solved?
   • What would be several acceptable outcomes?
   • What are the givens? List the aspects of the situation that cannot be changed.
   • What aspects of the situation might be flexible? List those aspects of the situation that can be changed.
   • How does the culture of the setting impact the situation? Make sure you consider this as you think about what can and cannot be changed and as you develop your action plan in the next section.

III. Action Plan
Think about the steps that would need to be taken in order to make the changes needed. List them in order here. Do this for each acceptable outcome.
   • Who are the players?
   • Who needs to be involved in discussion before anything can happen?
   • What is the best way for communication to take place?
   • What needs to happen first?
   • What do you need to do?

Worksheet on Changing the Physical Response to a Situation

A list of resources to help you learn techniques which may change your physical response to stressful situations can be found at the end of this chapter. Following are several of these techniques:

- meditation
- muscle relaxation
- yoga
- deep breathing
- exercise
- self-talk; repeating "stress-coping thoughts"
- nutrition
- self-hypnosis
- visualization
- biofeedback
- recording your own relaxation tape

Many of these ideas were adapted from Davis, Eshelman, and McKay (1995).

Worksheet for Cognitive Coping Skills

According to Cooley and Yovanoff (1996), the cognitive coping strategy involves changing how you think about a specific situation. It is based on literature on cognitive therapy and relies on the recognition of distorted beliefs and self or peer coaching to change one's way of thinking about a given situation. The following worksheet can be used as a guide to help you consider the beliefs involved in your interpretation of a given situation, and then to rethink or change those beliefs.

I. Describe the problem situation

- Who is involved?
- What is the nature of the problem? Describe clearly.
- Why is it a problem?
- How long has the situation been going on?

II. Recognition of various beliefs/ Changing or rethinking those beliefs

Think carefully about your interpretation of the problem situation.

- Are there other possible interpretations?
- Think of as many different reasons for the situation as possible.
- How do you view your role in the situation?
- How do you view the role and/or responsibility of other people?
- What are some other ways of viewing your role or responsibility for what is occurring?
- What are some other ways of viewing the role or responsibility of others?
- Is your interpretation of the situation rational?
- What are your irrational thoughts about the situation? "At the root of all irrational thinking is the assumption that things are done to you" (Davis et al, p.143).
- Is there evidence to support the irrational interpretation? If so, what is the evidence?
- List the evidence or facts of the situation. What are the rational interpretations which are possible?
- What are your emotions about the situation? Are they appropriate, given the facts?
- As you think about the facts of the situation in a rational, logical way, might you have different emotions, which might be more appropriate?
- What can you tell yourself to change your emotions or your interpretations of events or situations?

8.1 Exercise for Your Journal: Applying Coping Skills

Based on the three different coping skills or strategies described above (situational, physiological, and cognitive), develop different ways of coping with the stressful situations described in the following vignettes. Remember that a particular situation may lend itself better to one of the strategies than another. Use the worksheets to help guide you.

Vignette I : Working with an Aide

You are a recently certified special education teacher assigned to teach in a special education class where there is an aide, Mrs. Smith. She has been working in that class for the past 10 years with a teacher who became ill during the summer and cannot return. Since you were hired late, you have not had much time to learn about your students, your classroom, or the school. You have not had a chance to meet Mrs. Smith before the beginning of school.

On the first day, Mrs. Smith, who is your mother's age, is not overly friendly. She knows all the children because they were in the class last year, and they seem to be very attached to her. She also knows all the parents. When you try to talk about your expectations, the children seem to have expectations of their own, based on what has happened in the past. It is now the third week of school, and things have not improved. The children seem to regard her as the real teacher; they ask her questions and don't always listen to you. When parents drop off their children, they talk to Mrs. Smith, not to you. She has a friendly relationship with the parents; they rarely include you in their conversations. Mrs. Smith lives in the neighborhood, and her own children went to the school. She is well respected in the school and hasn't done anything to help you learn the ropes or meet people. You are becoming more and more discouraged. Some days you have to keep from bursting into tears in school. You are beginning to question your own ability to teach and to relate to parents. You find yourself going home and working very late every night, and you often cry yourself to sleep. What can you do to improve the situation?

Vignette II: The Teachers' Room

You are student teaching in a community next to the one where you grew up. You know several of the families of the children in the school. Your cooperating teacher suggests that you come into the Teachers' Room for lunch so that you will meet people. You look forward to this opportunity because you have felt somewhat isolated in the school, and you would like to observe in some classrooms other than the one in which you are teaching. You know that it is important for you to get to know some of the other teachers. You like your cooperating teacher and appreciate her efforts to help you. The other students in your weekly student teaching seminar at the college feel that you are very fortunate that you have a cooperating teacher who is trying to help you meet other people.

On the first day that you go into the Teachers' Room, you listen to the conversation and notice that most of the talk is about movies and books. The few comments that are made about children are mostly negative. A couple of teachers are complaining about the lack of cooperation of some of the children. You say very little, although you join in talking about movies that you have seen or books that you have read. On subsequent visits, you hear more conversation about children and their families. You are beginning to get increasingly uncomfortable with the tenor of the conversation. Some of the discussion about families sounds somewhat gossipy. You are finding it increasingly stressful to be in the Teachers' Room, but your cooperating teacher likes to go in there and continually talks about how important it is that you are meeting people. One day, a name is mentioned, and you realize that the parents being discussed are friends of your own parents. The teachers are making very unflattering comments about this family and the way they raise their children. You feel that, because you are a student teacher, it is best that you don't say anything, but you are very uncomfortable after that day. What can you do?

Vignette III: A Difficult Class

You spent last year in a year long internship as part of your Master's program and had a very positive experience. It is now the second month of school, and you are in your first year of teaching on your own in a third grade class. Your teacher preparation program was very strong in curriculum, but not so strong in behavior management. Before you began the year, you were quite confident about your teaching skills and had wonderful ideas, but now it seems that the class is in chaos. From the first day you entered the school, you have been hearing how difficult your class is. The second grade teacher told you that in the ten years that she has been teaching, she has never seen a group like this. Each teacher before her has had the same reaction. The custodian told you that he's been working in that school for 15 years and has never seen another group that is as badly behaved as this one. You haven't been able to teach the way you want to; you've been yelling at the children to get them to quiet down and pay attention. The principal has been coming into your room to observe you. She knew that you would have trouble and feels badly, but her suggestions haven't really helped so far. In spite of all the difficulties, however, you like most of the children and feel that there must be a way to reach them, so you are not ready to give up. You are getting stomachaches every morning and headaches at night though and don't know how much longer you can continue. How might you cope?

Support Groups

Colleges and school systems are beginning to offer support groups for new teachers. Student teaching seminars provide such support for pre-service teachers. The opportunity to sit with a group of peers who have been through or are currently experiencing similar types of problems can be very useful. Group problem-solving and sharing of experiences provides a vehicle for analyzing difficult situations and designing alternative approaches. The group may also energize you to go home and figure out answers for yourself, to do your own problem-solving.

SUMMARY

Teaching, though exciting and rewarding, can also be a stressful profession. In this chapter, we've attempted to help you to understand and recognize the symptoms of stress and burnout, as well as to guide you in thinking about various ways that you can decrease stress, avoid burnout, and find professional satisfaction. Some of these strategies are ones that you do by and for yourself, such as those related to taking care of yourself and limiting your commitments.

In addition to these ideas, gaining support from other educators can help ease the stresses caused by the social isolation which tends to occur during the first year of teaching and even during student teaching. It is helpful if your associations are with people who have an overall positive outlook on their work. Although you need the opportunity to air frustrations and to vent, ongoing gripe sessions will not be ultimately helpful and will only reinforce negative attitudes and increase stress. For more ideas about finding professional communities, refer to the next chapter.

Suggested Resources

Benson, H. (2000). *The relaxation response.* N.Y.: Harper Torch.

Borysenko, J. (1987). *Minding the body, mending the mind.* Reading, MA: Addison-Wesley.

Davis, M., Eshelman, E.,& McKay, M. (1995). *The relaxation and stress reduction workbook.* Oakland,CA: New Harbinger Publications.

Lakein A. (1974). *How to get control of your time and your life.* N.Y.: New American Library.

CHAPTER NINE

FINDING PROFESSIONAL COMMUNITIES AND NETWORKS

Throughout their careers, teachers should have ongoing opportunities to update their skills. In addition to time for joint planning and problem solving with in-school colleagues, teachers should have access to networks, school-university partnerships, and academies where they can connect with colleagues to study subject matter teaching, new pedagogies, and school change. These opportunities should offer sustained work on problems of practice that are directly connected to teachers' work and student learning. They should allow for in-depth inquiry, peer coaching, and sharing of knowledge so that real transformations of practice are possible. (National Commission on Teaching and America's Future, 1996, p. 21)

The importance of networking and of involvement in professional communities has been stated several times in this guide. They are intrinsic to becoming a professional teacher. Communities of colleagues are an invaluable resource as a vehicle for professional development and learning from others, as a way to facilitate self-reflection and examination of one's own teaching practices, and as a support to prevent burnout and stress. Opportunities for community can be found or created both within your school with colleagues there and outside of your school or school district with colleagues from other places. Some of these communities already exist within your school system and only have to be found. Others can be discovered outside of your school district, but may be easily accessible and readily useful to you. Some types of communities may actually be considered in both categories, but for discussion purposes we have divided them into one or another. Another type of group is one you create yourself with like-minded people who are within your school, outside your school, or some combination. This chapter will present descriptions of the different types of communities in which you may choose to participate.

First, we will discuss the many groups and organizations to which you will probably be introduced because they are affiliated with your school or district. These include school district professional development days and workshops, induction programs, unions, teacher associations, beginning teacher groups, parent/teacher organizations, professional development schools, and study groups.

Second, we will examine the kind of groups that are usually found outside the school district. Professional networks, student teaching seminars, and continuing education courses are possibilities if you are a student teacher or a beginning teacher near a college or university. Some kinds of groups can be formed with others in your school community with just a little organizational effort and a handful of people who are interested. This kind of group may be a support group, an informal network, or even an electronic support group or Internet chat room. These groups are less formally designed and may change over time, depending on the needs and interests of members. These kinds of groups require little or no commitment monetarily and exist only as needed. Some of these may appear to be unrelated directly to education but can still meet your personal and professional needs during the first year of teaching. Others may occur as outgrowths of relationships developed in the more formal structures in your school district.

FINDING PROFESSIONAL COMMUNITIES WITHIN YOUR SCHOOL SYSTEM

School District Professional Development Opportunities

School district-based professional development meets the needs of many teachers. As a first year teacher and often as a student teacher, you will undoubtedly attend district-based professional development days or half days when students are dismissed early. These are formatted to have lectures, workshops, and discussions for all teachers, regardless of experience. Often, experienced teachers who have a great deal to offer their peers lead these. Experience these as opportunities to work with and learn from your peers. If the days are one-size-fits-all, and don't seem to stimulate you, figure out how you can gain from these experiences anyway. One of the many advantages is that you will get to know your colleagues on a less formal basis. You can use the time together, before or after such sessions, to discuss issues of concern to you and seek help or make suggestions to others. Carpooling to central meeting places can provide you with the chance to chat with others briefly and make friends with colleagues who may otherwise seem too busy to offer friendship or mentoring during the school day.

9.1 Exercise for Your Journal: Share What You Know

As a student teacher or beginning teacher, you may want to share formally some state-of-the-art topic you have found useful and exciting in your recent coursework or student teaching seminar. Make a list of five projects or research papers you previously completed as part of your college coursework. Think broadly about your schooling and include classes beyond teacher education courses, especially those in content areas. If people in your school know of your interests, they may invite you, or if appropriate, you may offer to make a brief presentation or lead a discussion at a grade level or faculty meeting or as part of a professional development day. Before you make such an offer, you first should assess whether the culture of the school community views these offers for professional development positively.

Be active in seeking, encouraging, and organizing professional development opportunities that meet your needs. Here are some suggestions you may want to consider during your first or second year:

- ❑ Find out what professional development opportunities your system offers and how you can keep track of what's offered. Try to pencil these into your schedule in advance, so you don't miss out.
- ❑ Find out if you can attend local conferences that address areas you've been concerned with in your teaching.
- ❑ Let your principal, staff developers, and colleagues know of your interests so they can suggest activities they hear about.

Induction Programs

Many school systems are now offering formal induction programs which usually have several prescribed components. These components may be a series of professional development workshops before the school year begins, monthly meetings after school or on early release days, and an ongoing mentoring relationship. Topics for these workshops range from classroom management, differentiating curriculum, to working with parents and families. Such programs are mandated and partially funded by states such as California, where a set of teaching standards with specific goals and assessment benchmarks, provides guidelines for beginning teachers. Mentor activities and tasks may be standardized, with school districts directed to implement the details of the program and administer the funds locally. As we mentioned in the chapter on working with colleagues, mentoring gives you the opportunity to develop a special relationship with a more experienced teacher. In California, for example, two-stage certification provides for an ongoing plan of supervised professional development with clearly stated requirements for beginning teachers and mentors. Such programs are quite varied but are a valuable resource and source of support for many beginning teachers.

Unions and Teacher Organizations

If your school district is unionized, as most are, you will find colleagues in a different setting at union meetings and functions sponsored by professional organizations such as the American Federation of Teachers (AFT) or the National Education Association (NEA). As a student teacher, you can belong to one of the numerous student chapters of NEA at your college or university. These meetings give you another chance to get to know other teachers who are not at your school. You may find a mentor or new friend. These organizations typically offer workshops and events that may contribute to your professional development. Look for information regarding these opportunities on your staff room bulletin board. Many unions also offer new teacher support. Take advantage of the opportunity to network through organizations such as these.

> ### 9.2 Exercise for Your Journal:
>   Union Issues
>
> You may have joined your local teacher's union or you may be trying to decide if you will join. Whatever your decision, you will want to be informed about work actions that could affect you. You may need to make a decision regarding a union strike

or a work-to-rule action. These are a fact of life in teaching, and you may find yourself voting on such issues and perhaps participating. If you find your school or teacher's organization is involved in a work action, you will want to evaluate the pros and cons carefully.

Using the following questions, interview your building union representative, and take notes in your journal.

- How does the union support teachers in the system?
- What are the advantages of joining the union?
- What kinds of professional development opportunities does the union offer teachers?
- What does the union negotiating team do at contract renewal time and how does it involve its membership in decisions?
- Find out about the history of work actions in your school and school system.

Parent/Teacher Organizations (PTO)

Your school will most likely have a PTO, which could be an opportunity for professional development. The PTO is a group of parents and teachers who are working together for the success of the school and children. Projects often consist of extracurricular programs and fundraising to supplement the school activities and budget. Funds may be made available to teachers for supplies, equipment, or field trips. Activities could include special art or music performances, speakers, and visitors. Active participants usually constitute a small group of dedicated persons who can be stimulating and inspiring to work with. You will get to know some colleagues and a few parents well and can observe their perspective on education, the school, and goals for the children. This can be a very valuable learning experience for you. You can learn more about the culture of the school from experiences with the PTO. Teachers' participation and ideas about the PTO vary. Be attuned to the teacher's role in the PTO in your particular school setting.

You can choose how involved you want to be in the PTO. You can:

❏ be a teacher representative who attends and participates in

meetings and serves on committees,
- ❑ head up a project of special interest to you,
- ❑ just observe for the first few years,
- ❑ share what you've just learned about curriculum,
- ❑ share what you've just learned about child development,
- ❑ wait a couple of years to participate.

Professional Development Schools

The Professional Development School is a public or private school that has established a close relationship with the local college or university. The purposes of this relationship are to enhance the preparation of preservice teachers, enhance the professional development of veteran teachers, create opportunities for inquiry, and improve the education of children. If you are close to a college campus with a school of education, you may find yourself on the faculty of a Professional Development School. The Professional Development School is a place where practicing teachers can count on regular opportunities to grow personally and professionally. The best of these schools offer a climate that is supportive of renewal and conducive to ongoing learning. In these schools, teachers who are excited about their practice and looking for ways to improve can take advantage of workshops, courses, and study groups offered by the nearby college campus. The Professional Development School fosters collaboration between schools and colleges through teams of faculty and teachers who participate in joint seminars, action research groups, study groups, and other activities. The development of a network of colleagues that continues over time facilitates a culture of change and growth (Sears, 1992). The following vignettes are examples of activities of a Professional Development School partnership.

One university creates networks, opportunities for sharing ideas, and a culture of collegiality and change by having an annual or biannual mini-conference and dinner, bringing together faculty and administrators from all of their Professional Development Schools and partnership schools with faculty and administrators from the university. Teachers and other school staff are invited to present and facilitate roundtables and poster sessions. University liaisons, who are familiar with what is happening in the schools, individually encourage teachers and others to share their practice at the mini-conference. This encouragement and positive reinforcement has served to enhance the self-esteem and professional growth of participants, as well as to give people a chance to connect with each other. If new teachers aren't yet comfortable presenting, they can attend presentations or look at posters, participating when they are ready. The rooms buzz with excitement and conversation, both during sessions and during dinner. Teachers have borrowed ideas from colleagues at their own school or in other systems. Some have even been motivated to visit schools in other communities.

Several universities are part of a multi-university partnership with a Professional Development School district, committed to promoting a culture which values collegiality. Each university is paired with specific schools in the district, and representatives of all institutions meet regularly to plan and coordinate projects of the partnership. One of the universities offers an action research course on-site in a school, which includes both student teachers and veteran teachers from the schools. The participants engage in collaborative inquiry projects, which focus on their own interests and the needs of the system. The course provides a vehicle for networking, shared reflection, and collaborative professional development among preservice and veteran teachers and has helped to change the culture of the schools.

Study Groups

A study group provides for professional needs and will probably meet some of your personal needs as well. Such groups are often funded and sponsored by a college or your own school system. Talk to other teachers in your building or an administrator to find out if a study group exists that is of interest to you. A study group usually focuses on a particular topic, issue, or reviews a book or an article. The study group may rotate the group leader or facilitator along with the responsibilities for developing an agenda or calendar of meetings. Likely members of this kind of group could be experienced teachers or even administrators, as well as beginning teachers and student teachers. Study group members may also include teacher educators, psychologists, counselors, or other helping professionals whose work directly impacts children.

One successful study group met once a month at a local university. The teachers had a wide range of experiences and all had concerns about improving gender equity in their classrooms. They agreed to read a recently published research study and share their ideas about the issues and possible solutions. A grant paid for the reading materials and a light supper for each meeting. This group met after school and by the end of the evening, each individual was able to develop a list of strategies, which included long-term and immediate goals to be implemented in their respective classrooms.

FINDING PROFESSIONAL COMMUNITIES OUT-SIDE YOUR SCHOOL SYSTEM

Support Groups For Beginning Teachers

Some colleges organize support groups for their graduates who are first year teachers, such as the specially funded support group we conducted. Our support group met after school regularly, and although teachers said they were tired and that it was difficult to attend meetings because of their hectic schedules, they were always glad they made the time to be there once they actually arrived. The teaching support group can be a very satisfying way to stimulate your professional growth and to view issues in your particular school from a broader perspective. Moreover, it can provide a safer place to relax and problem solve away from the political environment of an individual school or Teachers' Room.

If you have no informal way of interacting regularly with other professionals that meets your needs, consider starting a teaching support group. The biggest advantage of this kind of group is that you can create the kind of group that you want. The groups can be developed around issues and practices you and your colleagues find useful to your teaching. This group can meet evenings or weekends, and you can gather for shop talk, problem solving, and socializing. Food helps. Order pizza or plan a potluck. Some teaching support groups continue for many years and include others who work with children, such as social workers or counselors. This group can be as small or large as you want and as formal or informal as you want. Draw from colleagues at your school, acquaintances, and former classmates. Try to include people from other school systems to give a broader range of perspectives.

> ### 9.3 Exercise for Your Journal:
> ### Who Will Be in Your Support Group?
>
> Imagine that you are going to start a support group. Spend some time writing down names and contact information of people in the categories listed below. A large group will dwindle as time goes by so err on the side of too many at the beginning. If you have time, you can find names, missing addresses and phone numbers on the Internet for those who may have moved.

Colleagues at your schools

Classmates and former classmates

Teachers from other school districts

Social workers (who work with children)

School counselors

Electronic Support Groups

Another kind of support group for beginning teachers can be found online through a computer network. With interactive networks available, you can communicate easily and frequently with other student teachers, beginning and experienced teachers, or administrators. One such network, based at the Harvard Graduate School of Education, was designed to link graduates of the Harvard teacher education program to faculty, staff, and a small number of second-year teachers who were involved in an online beginning teacher support group the previous year (Merseth, 1992). This kind of network is becoming more available to teachers and has the advantage of immediate availability of colleagues who otherwise are not easily reached for conversation and support because of distance.

The Internet offers endless possibilities for interacting with other professionals beyond electronic networks. Browsing the World Wide Web, you can get ideas and resources from other teachers. You can communicate individually with other teachers, create your own community group, and e-mail acquaintances you meet in person or on the web. You will find many sites of interest to you once you start to browse the web. If you need help getting started, try some of these sites, many of which are generated by teachers:

- ❏ Educast offers teachers a customized channel for access to various topics, articles, and lesson plans. *www.education.com*
- ❏ Kindergarten Connection offers articles, ideas and lesson plans. *www.kconnect.com*
- ❏ For lesson ideas and games that teach, try this website. *www.teachers.net*

❑ The New Teacher Center in Santa Cruz, CA is a national resource dedicated to teacher development and the support of programs and practices that promote excellence and diversity in America's teaching force. *www.newteachercenter.org*

❑ Nel Noddings is the author of this newsletter for teachers. The site includes over 180 links. *www.caringteachers.com*

❑ For abundant curriculum materials, teaching ideas and inspiration for K-12 math and science teaching and learning go to *www.enc.org*.

❑ The Association for Supervision and Curriculum Development offers a plethora of links for teachers' professional development. *www.ascd.org*

❑ This site offers hundreds of free standards-based activities, projects and resources for teachers and student teachers. *www.scholastic.com*

❑ Tales from the Electronic Frontier is a publication you can find online that features ten teachers' first-person accounts of using the Internet for lessons in both science and math. The site includes numerous resources and Web links: *www.wested.org/tales*

❑ Another way of using the Internet to connect with another professional is to submit a class question to Dr. Math: *www.mathforum.org/dr.math*
Students, teachers and classes are invited to submit questions that are intriguing to them. Graduate students, under the tutelage of several math professors, answer these questions. Occasionally the questions and their answers will cause debate among other experts. It certainly can be a lot of fun when your classroom's question gets posted.

❑ The Dr. Math site is part of an excellent Internet resource called the Math Forum *www.mathforum.org*. The Math Forum is filled with puzzles, reviews, curriculum ideas and games for grades K through 12. There is something for everyone here, and the puzzles can be easily downloaded.

❑ For all of you Tesselmaniacs check out the "HyperStudio and Rotation Tessellations" link: *www.mathforum.org/sum95/suzanne/grant/*
What is especially attractive about this one is that it includes a chapter called "Where's the Math?" which goes into some detail of the math in tessellations. Sites like these

can be found for most subject matter areas in elementary and middle school.

Go to the Internet to get lists and guides of interesting education sites and web pages. You can access information and websites for teachers using a search engine such as Google or Yahoo. You will find lists by subject like math and science, or you can search for topics such as multicultural curriculum or children's literature. These will take you to appropriate sites with simply a subject or word typed in for category. The web sites you may visit will offer you a plethora of background information, outlines and lesson plans, and will help you develop curriculum ideas focused on subjects such as social studies, science, language arts, and mathematics. Whatever your facility with computers, make a conscious effort to develop your skills in using the Internet as a resource. Set this as a goal for yourself, and note it in your journal.

Access the World Wide Web through any computer that connects with the Internet through a commercial or educational account. Look for free access in your school media center, city library, state college or university or for a fee, a computer service center. The World Wide Web opens infinite doors to student teachers and beginning teachers and any others seeking knowledge and support.

Professional Organizations

Join a professional organization such as the national associations for reading, math, special education, or early childhood teachers. These groups are not only for experienced professionals. Most of these organizations have reasonable student rates and may have student chapters you can join as a full time student. The national and regional organizations offer monthly journals, newsletters, regional and national conferences; students and teachers volunteering to assist at conferences may receive a stipend toward travel and hotel expenses. Always watch for conferences that are meeting near you so you can attend at minimal expense, such as a small registration fee. Becoming involved in an organization as a student may help you develop lifelong colleagues. Affiliation with a professional organization helps keep you updated in a field of interest. Skimming a professional publication each month can generate new ideas and may challenge your thinking about a particular classroom practice. Attending a conference or workshop takes extra time and effort you may think you do not have, but it is worthwhile. This is especially true if other teachers from your school are attending or encourage you to attend, and your school gives you time off and perhaps subsidizes your attendance. As one veteran teacher told us:

> I joined my state professional organization for technology teachers early in my career as a teacher. The information I obtained from reading the journal and newsletter kept me up-to-date in the profession and provided a quick and easy way to stay current in the field. Later in my teaching career, when I began to attend the annual conference regularly and participated in a special interest group, I found networking with other educators doing the same thing that I was and sharing ideas with colleagues from other districts, to be an invaluable part of my professional growth. After a number of years of teaching, I took a leadership role in the organization, chairing a committee and serving on the board. Being part of this collegial community, which connected me to many professionals across the state, has contributed tremendously to my professional growth, has been rejuvenating when I needed a dose of renewal, and has helped me contribute in new ways to my own school system. Being connected to a professional organization has helped me in every stage of my career as a teacher.

A list of contact information for some of these organizations is at the end of this chapter.

Professional Networks

A professional network is another way to stimulate your professional development and meet others with similar goals and interests. Participating in a network will offer you the opportunity to extend and deepen your classroom expertise while at the same time making or renewing friendships. You will be able to participate in a variety of activities and meet diverse participants if you become a part of a network. For example, the Puget Sound Educational Consortium (Lieberman & McLaughlin, 1992), a school/university partnership between the University of Washington and several school districts in Seattle, began with a group of teachers working on an action research project to investigate dimensions of teacher leadership. This project led to other teacher-directed activities, including presenting at conferences and developing and submitting successful proposals for grants to support future initiatives. Collaboration of this kind is stimulating and rewarding, both personally and professionally. This particular consortium stimulated critical reflection on practice and facilitated the collaborative construction of new roles for teachers.

Subject-matter collaboratives such as the Urban Mathematics Collaborative and the National Writing Project (Lieberman & McLaughlin, 1992; Little & McLaughlin, 1993) were created to support teaching and learning in a particular domain. These collaboratives involve teachers and others who are interested or actively involved in the field in other ways. If you choose to belong to such a group, you will meet others who are looking to review and explore content and methods that enhance their teaching, and improve classroom learning narrowed to a defined discipline. You will have a chance to learn from and share with teachers who have all kinds of experiences and backgrounds.

Networks that consist of members from different schools and districts allow educators to question each other, ask for help, or discuss realities without being afraid to expose themselves to their daily colleagues. These networks can lend validity to the experiences of educators and affirm both the importance of asking questions and the reality of the ambiguity of the teaching/learning process. Members can work together to solve problems and develop plans. The structure of networks can take many forms, from dinners to study groups, to mini-conferences to electronic networks. The existence of networks influences the culture of an organization by increasing openness, sharing, and thus the possibilities for collaborative inquiry and problem solving.

Networks usually have a clear focus, if not on subject matter, then on a specific project focusing on a trend or philosophy with identified goals and objectives. You will be able to dialogue with other professionals and perhaps try out techniques and ideas, followed by time for reflection, and collaborative assessment of the practice. You will have leadership opportunities that you may consider embracing after two or three years of teaching. These leadership opportunities may include influencing the focus and direction of the network, long term and short-term goal setting, and identifying likely members. If there is such a network in your community, you have much to gain from becoming involved.

Colleges and Universities

Colleges and universities offer traditional opportunities that are almost endless. Besides regular courses, if you are fortunate enough to live near a campus or satellite, you can take advantage of institutes, conferences, and workshops. Employed teachers sometimes receive a discount on tuition and fees for continuing education credits. Students often get discounted rates for conferences. A one-credit course or two-day conference or workshop could offer insight, information, and an opportunity to engage in collegial discussions and possibly make new friends. We advise keeping these course or workshop loads light for the first few years of teaching as you face the challenges of your new job. Three-credit courses and larger commitments are possibly too demanding for the beginning teacher. You don't want to add to your stress or frustration by taking on too much during your first year or two. You may want to eventually consider enrolling in a Master's program, which offers the advantage of a cohort of fellow students who can be sources of ongoing support.

Student Teaching Seminar and College Courses

Some of the best sources of professional relationships begin in your training experiences. Through your college courses and field experiences, as you complete requirements for certification, you will meet and interact regularly with a group of colleagues. Fostering and building on these relationships over time may give you a rich professional network. From working together on group projects and participating in classroom debates, role-plays, and reflective activities, you can get to know a group of colleagues well. Be assertive in developing these relationships even if you feel shy or hesitant. A golden learning opportunity may be awaiting among your multicultural classmates! You may be drawn to those who are more like you in immediately observable ways, but try also to develop relationships with those who appear to be unlike you. Following are some suggestions for making the most of your classes and helping you to develop your professional network.

- ❏ Consciously reaching out to others will help you to broaden your own knowledge and interpersonal experiences. You may get to know more about languages, cultures, beliefs, values, and traditions other than your own.
- ❏ As you obtain jobs in differing school districts after student teaching, you can continue to provide professional support to one another.
- ❏ Obtain peer phone numbers, addresses, and e-mail information for reference during and after your coursework.
- ❏ Talk with your colleagues about issues discussed in your classes. These conversations can help you to develop your

own opinions, personal style, approach to teaching, and enrich your understanding of the issues.
❑ Take advantage of all opportunities for collaborative work in your courses and try to create them when possible. Conventional wisdom suggests that collaboration for pre-service and in-service teachers is almost always an advantage to learning and professional development.

All of these activities will increase the probability that you will reach out to your colleagues in your new school.

SUMMARY

There are many kinds of professional communities and networks with different purposes, a number of which we have called to your attention. The opportunity to share information, ideas, and resources can reduce feelings of stress that occur by being isolated as you struggle through the challenges of the first few years of teaching. A proactive decision to become part of a network can enhance feelings of control. Participation in a professional community can be a vehicle for allowing you to assume new roles, develop professionally, and influence the world beyond your classroom.

Professional Organizations

American Federation of Teachers
555 New Jersey Ave. N.W.
Washington, D.C. 20001

Association for Supervision and
Curriculum Development
1250 North Pitt Street
Alexandria, VA. 22314

Council for Exceptional Children
1920 Association Drive
Reston, Virginia 20191-1589

International Reading Association
800 Barksdale Road
P. O. Box 8139
Newark, DE. 19714-8139

National Education Association
1201 16th St. N.W.
Washington, D.C. 20036

National Association for the Education of Young Children
1509 16th Street, NW
Washington, DC 20036-1426

National Association for Multicultural Education
733 15th St. N.W., Suite 430
Washington, D. C. 20005

National Council for the Social Studies
3501 Newark Street N. W.
Washington, D. C. 20016

National Council of Teachers of English
1111 Kenyon Road
Urbana, IL. 61801

National Council of Teachers of Mathematics
1906 Association Drive
Reston, VA. 22091

National Science Teachers Association
1742 Connecticut Avenue N.W.
Washington D. C. 20009-1171

Phi Delta Kappa International
408 N. Union
P. O. Box 789
Bloomington, IN 47402-0789

EPILOGUE

So now that you've read this book, what have you learned? We hope, of course, that you've learned some ideas that will help you in not only adjusting to your beginning years of teaching, but also in feeling satisfaction and experiencing professional growth. We hope that, if you didn't understand before, you now see that you can make your classroom a better environment for your students if your school is a better workplace for you. As we've said in many different ways throughout this book, we believe that you can enhance the environment for both yourself and your students if you interact with and utilize a broad range of resources from the larger community, both inside and outside of your school.

If nothing else, we hope we've helped you see how complex this profession of teaching really is. We hope that we've given you some tools to help you deal with the complexities and to be the master of your own fate. We've repeatedly stressed the importance of collegiality. Your colleagues will help you develop your own competence and your sense of comfort in your chosen profession.

If you assumed that all you'd have to think about would be the children in your classroom, you now must see that the often unexplained part of becoming a teacher is learning how to relate to, and work, with other adults — colleagues, staff, parents, and administrators. From this understanding flows your ultimate satisfaction and growth. You'll feel less isolated in your school. You'll have someone to turn to if things get out of control. You'll learn strategies and ideas from what others know. Remember, it's the people that matter!

We hope that this book will help you as you continue on your professional journey as an educator, both learning from and teaching others along the way. We wish you many years of successful teaching, many wonderful colleagues, and the joy of finding satisfaction in important work that you love!

Marcia Bromfield

Harriet Deane

Ella Glenn Burnett

REFERENCES

Aiken, L. (1972). Research on attitudes toward mathematics. *Arithmetic Teacher,* *19,* 229-234.

Ann Arbor Public Schools (1993). *Alternative assessment: Evaluating student performance in elementary mathematics.* Palo Alto, CA: Dale Seymour Publications.

Armstrong, T. (2000). *Multiple intelligences in the classroom.* Alexandria, VA: Association for Supervision and Curriculum Development.

Ayers, W. (1995). Becoming a teacher: Making a difference in children's lives. In W. Ayers (Ed.), *To become a teacher* (pp.5-9). New York: Teachers College Press.

Bambino, D. (2002). Critical friends. *Educational Leadership, 59* (6), 25-27.

Barbour, C. & Barbour, N. (1997). *Families, schools, and communities.* Upper Saddle Creek, NJ: Prentice Hall.

Barth, R. (1990). *Improving schools from within.* San Francisco: Jossey-Bass.

Barth, R. (1996). School and university: Bad dreams, good dreams. *On common ground: Strengthening teaching through school-university partnership.* 6, 1; 5-7.

Berger, E. H. (2000). *Parents as partners in education: Families and schools working together* (5th ed.). Upper Saddle River, NJ: Merrill.

Budoff, M. (1999). Models of co-teaching. In S. Graham & K.R. Harris (Eds.), *Teachers working together: Enhancing the performance of students with special needs* (pp. 214-231). Cambridge, MA: Brookline Books.

Brock, B.L. & Grady, M.L. (1997). *From first-year to first-rate.* Thousand Oaks, CA: Corwin.

Busher, H., Clarke, S., & Taggart, L. (1988). Beginning teachers' learning. In J. Calderhead (Ed.), *Teachers' professional learning* (pp. 84-96). London: Routledge Falmer.

Campbell, D.M., Cignetti, P.B., Melenyzer, B.J., Nettles, D.H., & Wyman, Jr., R.M. (1997). *How to develop a professional portfolio: A manual for teachers.* Needham Heights, MA: Allyn & Bacon.

Chall, J. S., Bissex, G., Conard, S., & Harris-Sharples, S. (1996). *Qualitative assessment of text difficulty: A practical guide for teachers and writers.* Cambridge, MA: Brookline Books.

Children's Defense Fund (2000). *The state of America's children.* Washington, D.C: Author.

Cherniss, C. (1980). *Professional burnout in human service organizations.* New York: Praeger.

Clay, M. (1993). *An observational survey of early literacy achievement.* Auckland, NZ: Heinemann.

Coleman, M. (1991). Planning for the changing nature of family life in schools for young children. *Young Children, 46*(4), 15-20.

Cooley, E. & Yovanoff, P. (1996). Supporting professionals-at-risk: Evaluating interventions to reduce burnout and improve retention of special educators. *Exceptional Children, 62,* (4), 336-355.

Danzberger, J., Bodinger-deUriarte, C., & Clark, M. (1996). *A guide to promising practices in educational partnerships.* Washington, D.C.: U.S. Department of Education, Office of Educational Research and Improvement.

Darling-Hammond, L. (1998). Teacher learning that supports student learning. *Educational Leadership, 55* (5), 6-11.

Davis, M., Eshelman, E., & McKay, M. (1995). *The relaxation and stress reduction workbook.* Oakland, CA: New Harbinger Publications.

Delprete, T. (1997). The "rounds" model of professional development. *From the Inside,* 1, 13-14.

Dryfoos, J. G. (1996). Full-service schools. *Educational Leadership, 53* (7), 18-23.

Emig, J. (1977). Writing as a mode of learning. *College Composition and Communication, 28* (2), 122-28.

Epstein, J.L. (1986). Parents' reactions to teacher practices of parent involvement. *The Elementary School Journal, 86* (3), 277-294.

Epstein, J.L. (1995). School/family/community partnerships: Caring for the children we share. *Phi Delta Kappan, 76* (9), 701-712.

Epstein, J.L. & Dauber, S.L. (1991). School programs and teacher practices of parent involvement in inner-city elementary and middle schools. *The Elementary School Journal, 91* (3), 289-305.

Evans, C. (1991). Support for teachers studying their own work. *Educational Leadership, 28* (6), 11-13.

Feiman-Nemser, S. & Floden, R. E. (1986). The cultures of teaching. In M. C. Wittrock (Ed.), *Handbook of research on teaching.* (3rd ed.), (pp 505-526). New York: Macmillan Publishing Company.

Finders, M. and Lewis, C. (1994). Why some parents don't come to school. *Educational Leadership, 51* (8) p. 50-54.

Fisher, R. & Ury, W. (1981). *Getting to yes.* New York: Penguin Books.

Flagg St.-Assumption College (n.d.). PDS brochure.

Fleming, D.S. (2000). How teachers look at student work together. *PDS Listserv.* Retrieved October 7, 2000, from http://Pds_devel@nici-mc2.org

Freiberg, H.J. (1995). Promoting reflective practice. In G.A. Slick (Ed.): *Emerging trends in teacher preparation: The future of field experiences* (pp. 25-42). Thousand Oaks, CA: Corwin.

Fried, R.L. (1995). *The passionate teacher.* Boston, MA: Beacon Press.

Friend, M. & Cook, L. (1996). *Interactions: Collaboration skills for school professionals* (2nd ed.). White Plains, NY: Longman Publishers.

Fullan, M. & Hargreaves, A. (1996). *What's worth fighting for in your school?* New York: Teachers College Press.

Galinsky, E. (1987). *The six stages of parenthood.* Reading, MA: Addison-Wesley.

Gardner, H. (1983). *Frames of mind: The theory of multiple intelligences.* New York: Basic Books.

Gersten, J. (1992). Families in poverty. In M. Procidano & C. Fisher (Eds.). *Contemporary families: A handbook for school professionals* (pp. 137-158). New York: Teacher's College Press.

Gestwiecki, C. (1996). *Home, school and community relations: A guide to working with parents* (3rd ed.). Albany, NY: Delmar Publishers.

Guillaume, A.M. & Yopp, H.K. (1995). Professional portfolios for student teachers. *Teacher Education Quarterly, 22* (1), 93-101.

Halaby, M.H. (2000). *Belonging: Creating community in the classroom.* Cambridge, MA: Brookline Books.

Harvard Elementary School (1995). School Improvement Plan. Harvard, MA.

Henderson, A.T. (Ed.). (1987). *The evidence continues to grow.* Columbia, MD: National Committee for Citizens in Education.

Hopkins, D. (1993). *A teacher's guide to classroom research* (2nd ed.). Bristol, PA: Open University Press.

Hubbard, R.S. & Power, B.M. (1993). *The art of classroom inquiry.* Portsmouth, NH: Heinemann.

Hulseboch, P.L. (1992). Significant others: Teachers' perspectives on relationships with parents. In W.H. Schubert & W.C. Ayers (Eds.), *Teacher Lore: Learning from our own experience* (pp.107-132). White Plains, NY: Longman.

Jackson, P.W. (1968). *Life in classrooms.* New York: Holt, Rinehart, & Winston.

Johnson, D., Johnson, R., & Holubec, E. (2002). *Circles of learning* (5th ed.). Edina, MN: Interaction Books.

Johnson, M. & Kress, R. (1997). *Informal reading inventories* (3rd ed.). Newark, DE: International Reading Association.

Johnson, S.M. (1990). *Teachers at work: Achieving success in our schools.* New York: Basic Books.

Johnson, S.M. & Kardos, S.M. (2002). Keeping new teachers in mind. *Educational Leadership, 59* (6), 12-16.

Kelly, K. (2002). Lesson study: Can Japanese methods translate to U.S. schools? *Harvard Education Letter, 18* (3), 4-7.

Killion, J.P. & Todnem, G.R. (1991). A process for personal theory building. *Educational Leadership, 28* (6), 14-16.

Knoblock, P. & Goldstein, A. (1971). *The lonely teacher.* Boston: Allyn and Bacon.

Lieberman, A. & McLaughlin, M.W. (1992). Network for educational change: Powerful and problematic. *Phi Delta Kappan, 73* (9), 673-677.

Lieberman, A. & Miller, L. (1992). *Teachers: Their world and their work.* New York: Teachers College Press.

Lightfoot, S.L. (1978). *Worlds apart.* New York: Basic Books.

Little, J.W. & McLaughlin, M.W. (1993). *Urban math collaboratives: As the teacher tells it.* Stanford, CA: Center for Research on the Context of Secondary School Teaching.

Loucks-Horsley, S., Harding, C.K., Arbuckle, M.A., Murray, L.B., Dubea, C., & Williams, M.K. (1987). *Continuing to learn: A guidebook for teacher development.* Andover, MA: The Regional Laboratory for Educational Improvement of the Northeast and the Islands.

Lynch, E.W. & Hanson, M.J. (1998). *Developing cross-cultural competence* (2nd ed.). Baltimore, MD: Paul H. Brookes Publishing Co.

Maslach, C. (1982). *Burnout: the cost of caring.* Englewood Cliffs, NJ: Prentice-Hall.

Maeroff, G. (1998). *Altered destinies: Making life better for schoolchildren in need.* New York: St. Martin's Press.

MathSteps (2000). Boston: Houghton Mifflin.

McMackin, M. (n.d.). Portfolio handouts. Cambridge, MA: Lesley University.

Merseth, K.K. (1992). First aid for first-year teachers. *Phi Delta Kappan, 92* (9), 678-682.

Metzger, M. & Fox, C. (1986). Two teachers of letters. *Harvard Educational Review, 56* (4), 349-354.

Morrow, R.D. (1987). Cultural differences—be aware! *Academic Therapy, 23* (2), 143-149.

National Commission on Teaching and America's Future. (1996). *What matters most: Teaching for America's future.* New York: Author.

National Council of Teachers of Mathematics (2000). *Principles and standards.* Reston, VA: Author.

Ogle, D.M. (1986). K-W-L: A teaching model that develops active reading of expository text. *Reading Teacher, 39* (6), 564-570.

Pasch, S.H. & Pugach, M.C. (1990). Collaboration: Empowering educators to take charge. *Contemporary Education, 61* (3), 135-143.

Pollard, A. & Tann, S. (1987). *Reflective teaching in the primary school.* London: Cassell.

Reinhiller, N. (1996). Co-teaching: New variations on a not-so-new practice. *Teacher Education and Special Education 19* (1), 34-48.

Rosenholtz, S.J. & Kyle, S.J. (1984). Teacher isolation: Barriers to professionalism. *American Educator, 8* (4), 10-15.

Saphier, J. (n.d.). *Presentation on Core Values.* Newton, MA.

Sarason, S. (1996). *Revisiting "The culture of the school and the problem of change."* New York: Teachers College Press.

Sears, A. (1992). Buying back your soul: Restoring ideals in social studies teaching. *Social Studies and the Young Learner, 4* (3), 9-11.

Shanker, E. & Ekwall, J. (1999). *Ekwall/Shanker reading inventory* (4th ed.). Needham Heights, MA: Allyn & Bacon.

Swap, S.M. (1987). *Enhancing parent involvement in schools.* New York: Teacher's College Press.

Swap, S.M. (1993). *Developing home-school partnerships: From concepts to practice.* New York: Teacher's College Press.

Tama, M.C. & Peterson, K. (1991). Achieving reflectivity through literature. *Educational Leadership, 28* (6), 22-24.

Tickle, L. (1994). *The induction of new teachers: Reflective professional practice.* London: Cassell.

Underwood School (1993). Core Values Statement. Newton, MA.

Watanabe, T. (2002). Learning from Japanese lesson study. *Educational Leadership, 59* (6), 36- 39.

Webb, R.B. & Sherman, R.R. (1989). *Schooling and society* (2nd ed.). New York: MacMillan Publishing Company.

Weiss, H.B. (1997). Rewards of engaging families in children's education. *The Boston Globe*, December 7, G15 (3rd edition Learning section)

Wildman, T.M., Magliaro, S.G., Niles, R.A. & Niles, J. A. (1992). Teacher mentoring: An analysis of roles, activities, and conditions. *Journal of Teacher Education (43)* 3, 205-213.

Yellin, D. & Blake, M.E. (1994). *Integrating the language arts: A holistic approach.* New York: Harper Collins.

Yopp, H. (1996). A test for assessing phonemic awareness in young children. *The Reading Teacher,* 49 (1), 20-29.

INDEX

ABOUT THE AUTHORS

MARCIA BROMFIELD has been Associate Professor and Director of Field Placement and Professional Partnerships in the School of Education at Lesley University for the past 20 years. She has been involved in teacher preparation in higher education for 28 years and prior to that worked in special education. She received her B.A. from Tufts University and her Ph.D. from Syracuse University. Marcia has published and done presentations in a variety of areas related to special education, teacher preparation, school/college partnerships, and support for beginning teachers.

HARRIET DEANE is Assistant Professor and Assistant Dean in the School of Education at Lesley University. She received her B.A. from Washington University, her M.Ed. from Boston University, and her M.B.A. from the Simmons Graduate School of Management. Harriet has taught middle school English and early childhood education in urban and suburban settings. Her interests include family/school/community collaboration, beginning teacher support and teacher preparation.

ELLA GLENN BURNETT is a Professor in the College of Education at California State University, Long Beach. She earned her Bachelor's and Master's degrees from Pittsburg State University. She has a doctorate from UCLA. She has taught middle school math and elementary school in urban and suburban districts. She has published articles and book chapters in the areas of mathematics education, professional development, and teacher induction into diverse classrooms.